ESS

WALKS FOR MOTORISTS

Fred Matthews
&
Wm. A. Bagley

30 Walks with sketch maps

COUNTRYSIDE BOOKS
NEWBURY, BERKSHIRE

Countryside Books' walking guides cover most areas of England and Wales and include the following series:

County Rambles
Walks For Motorists
Exploring Long Distance Paths
Literary Walks
Pub Walks

A complete list is available from the publishers

First Published 1977
by Frederick Warne Ltd
This completely revised and updated edition
published 1992
Reprinted 1994

COUNTRYSIDE BOOKS
3 Catherine Road
Newbury, Berkshire

ISBN 1 85306 174 3

Cover photograph: Thaxted Mill and Church taken by Andy Williams.

Publishers' Note

At the time of publication all footpaths used in these walks were designated as official footpaths or rights of way, but it should be borne in mind that diversion orders may be made from time to time.

Although every care has been taken in the preparation of this Guide, neither the Author nor the Publisher can accept responsibility for those who stray from the Rights of Way.

Produced through MRM Associates Ltd., Reading
Typeset by Wessex Press Design & Print Limited, Warminster
Printed in England by J. W. Arrowsmith Ltd., Bristol

Contents

Introduction

I am very grateful to have been given the opportunity to revise and update my late friend William Bagley's book. In order to preserve the spirit of his work, I have left the introductions to his walks mainly untouched. His style shows what a great author and lover of the countryside he was. He will be remembered for the pleasure he has given to all walkers who follow his routes.

On these walks you will find great variety, including the Essex Green Lanes. All the walks are circular and are on rights of way or permissive paths.

The sketch maps are intended to make it easy to find the start of the walk and to give a general idea of the route to be taken. For those who like the benefit of more detailed maps, the relevant Ordnance Survey 1:50,000 Landranger maps are given at the start of each walk.

The following symbols will help you to interpret the sketch maps:

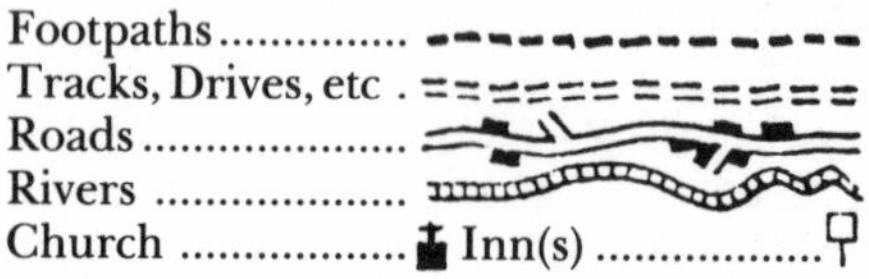

Footpaths ....
Tracks, Drives, etc .
Roads ....
Rivers ....
Church .... Inn(s) ....

No special equipment is needed to enjoy the countryside on foot, but do wear a stout pair of shoes and remember that at least one muddy patch is likely even on the sunniest day. Do remember the Country Code and make sure gates are not left open nor any farm animals disturbed.

I would like to put on record the help received from two good companions of the footpath way Colin R. Hills and A. Geoffrey Stevenson. I would also like to add my thanks to all my colleagues who have assisted me in the revisions for this new edition, particularly Derek Davies, Bill Linnell and Marjorie Haylock — truly a cooperative effort.

Many hours of enjoyment have gone into the preparation of these walks. I hope you will enjoy them too. To use William Bagley's own words 'Meet the challenge! Have fun! May you enjoy fine weather and good companionship'.

Fred Matthews

Area map showing locations of the walks.

WALK 1

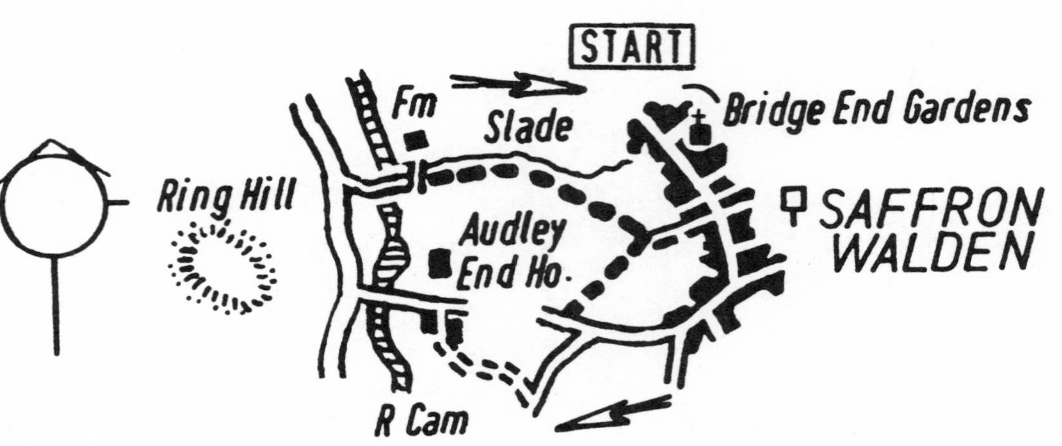
START
Bridge End Gardens
SAFFRON
WALDEN
Fm
Slade
Ring Hill
Audley
End Ho.
R Cam

SAFFRON WALDEN AND AUDLEY END (LION GATE)

WALK 1

★

4 miles (6.4 km)

OS Landranger 154

This is a walk designed to fit in with a visit to Audley End — the noblest house in all Essex — and to attractive old Saffron Walden.

Audley End House is said to have cost quite £200,000 — a great deal of money in the 1600s. The story goes that when King James I came down to see the work in progress he acidly remarked to the crafty Thomas Howard, the Lord Treasurer for whom the house was being built: 'It is too much for a King but it might do very well for a Lord Treasurer.'

In this democratic age however, the house is now in the care of the Department of the Environment.

Saffron Walden is as charming as its name. At one time the growing of saffron (yellow crocus) was so much a local industry that it gave the town the first part of its name. The deep-orange powder was once extensively used for colouring and flavouring certain foods, eg rice. Nowadays it is mostly used by the more exotic television and newspaper cooks, at least as far as this county goes.

Saffron Walden is reached by driving north along the B1383 from Newport and beyond the turning for Audley End House taking the signposted road on the right to the town. At the T-junction turn right along the high street to turn right at the traffic lights. Bear left, soon passing the common on your right. Beyond the common go over crossroads and take the second road on the left signposted to a car park and park on the left beside the football ground.

From the car park continue ahead through Bridge End Gardens and at the end of the green turn right onto a path leading into the gardens. Time should be taken to visit the gardens (say an hour or so) which contain an art gallery and a newly open hedged maze. Just inside the entrance to the gardens turn left on a path on the left edge of the gardens back to the main road where you turn left. Pass the Eight Bells public house and turn right on Freshwell Street. Continue with a flint wall on your left and at the end of a field on the right turn left to turn right into Prince's Close. Pass under an arch and follow the path to a road where you turn right to the gates into Audley End House grounds. Continue ahead on a straight stoney path running uphill to a lodge.

Go through a gate into a lane. Turn left for 100 yards. At a junction turn rightwards along another lane downhill to a copse. Here take the track on the right to Abbey Farm.

Just past the farm the track bends to the right and you continue along it noting the almshouses over on the left. At a junction continue ahead to enter the hamlet of Audley End. The house can be seen behind the wall. You come to a lane and turning left soon come to the Lion Gate entrance to Audley End House.

If you intend to visit the house you can of course use the extensive car park and start the walk from here but note closing times and check whether it is in order to re-enter the car park on foot without further fee if you have left the park to go for a stroll outside.

Continue ahead onto the bridge over the river Cam and on to the main road in which you turn rightwards. This way you soon get a more leisurely view, over the ha-ha (a kind of dry moat), of the west front of Audley End House than you would if speeding along in a car with your attention otherwise engaged.

Before reaching a lodge on the right, glance leftwards up a hillside. A domed temple will be observed at the northern edge of woodland (which itself covers an ancient camp).

Continue along the road past the (Cambridge) lodge just mentioned and along by the flint wall which follows.

At the end of this turn rightwards on to the drive of Home Farm. Follow this, noting the obelisk behind the farm, back over the Cam. Where the drive bends left, over a stream, to farm buildings, go *rightwards* to continue alongside the flint wall that has been on your right.

Soon you come out into a meadow. Go ahead across this with a stream (the Slade) on your left and another view of the House over to your right. There is a pillared temple to its left.

At the end of the meadow an enclosed path leads past a 'Works'. Beyond this continue through a field (I was glad to find, on my visit, that an unploughed strip had been retained) to a lodge.

Bear left through a gate into the road, bearing right with the road, with a flint wall on your right. Pass a no entry sign and continue on to and over the main road at a traffic light. Beyond the toilets on your right, turn left onto an arcade leading to a road where you then turn right to a T-junction.

Turn left to the market square, then turn left past the information centre. At the end of the market turn right with the town hall on the left and the market on the right. Continue uphill and at the crossroads note the bookshop on the left. Go over a crossroads to the entrance to the museum and castle on your right and then turn left into the churchyard with the church on your left. Continue past the grave of the former Education Minister R. A. Butler who introduced the 1944 Education Act and beyond the church turn right on a narrow passage to a road where you turn left for 5 yards then right onto a path signposted for Bridge End Gardens. On the green turn right to reach the car park.

NEWPORT AND DEBDEN

WALK 2

★

5, 6 or 8 miles (8, 9.5 or 13 km)

OS Landranger 154, 167

The basic walk is an easy 5 miles. A detour into Debden village would add a mile and further detour via Purton End would add another 2 miles.

This is not the type of country to hustle through and there is much of interest to see and to photograph. I have, in my main text, hinted at such interesting things as Newport Toll House, Debden church and the Milestone in the Wood.

Newport is on the main Cambridge B1383 road 40 miles from Central London.

Parking spaces can be found at odd places about the village, but park discreetly. There is usually some space to be found in front of the railway station or at the north end of the village by turning right just beyond the Toll House (on the left of the main road) and passing under the viaduct where space can be found on the right beyond the highways depot (beware river on far side of parking space).

At Newport station cross the railway line by the public footbridge to the lane beyond, along which you must then turn rightwards. Where the lane ends at the entrance (on the right) to a chalk pit continue ahead uphill on a hedged green lane. Towards the top of the hill the hedges end and the path becomes a field edge track with fine all-round views leading ahead along the top of the ridge to a lane elbow. Go leftwards along this for 100 yards or so.

Where the lane soon bears left continue forward on a firm track which a nameboard indicates leads to Waldegraves Farm. Continue on the track past the farm going on to walk alongside a wood. Shortly where the footpath from Widdington comes in from the right, fork half left on a wide track downhill into the wood. The path goes round bends then comes out to run between fields with views of Debden church away to the right.

Towards the end of the fields disregard a footpath sign inviting you to go leftwards. Instead, continue over a bridge, point W, which spans a narrow arm of Debden Park lake. Immediately beyond (in front of a farm building) turn off rightwards on to an enclosed path.

This leads to a meadow. Continue across this, past a 'pudding-stone' to the church — an 18th century Gothic structure albeit of medieval foundation which is as interesting inside as it is out. I was most agreeably

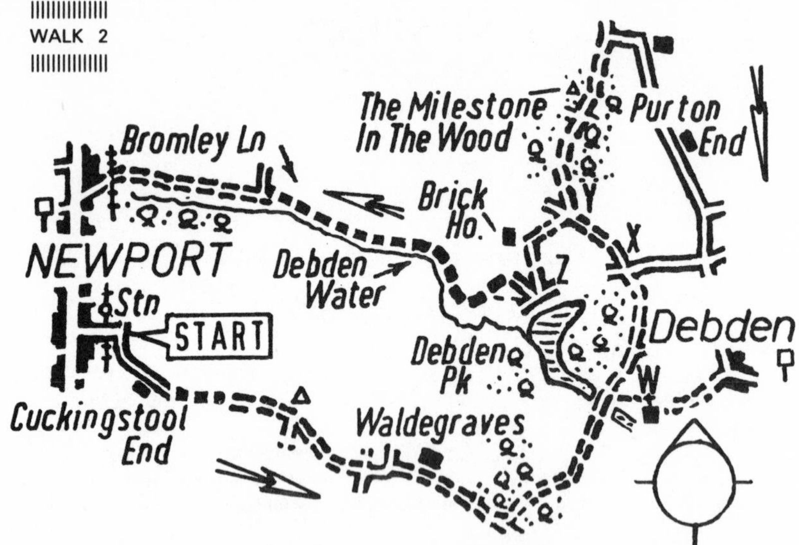

surprised, on my visit, to find the remote church unlocked and unattended.

If you now wish to visit Debden village (about 2½ miles from the start) for an inn or just to look round, continue in the church drive. Afterwards retrace your way to point W and turn rightwards as though you had not taken the church/village detour but had kept straight on over the little bridge.

The winding track soon forks and you take the leftward branch, disregarding the rightward approach to Hall Farm. You go along an avenue and then through a belt of trees to a road by a former lodge. (Debden Hall was demolished in 1936 and some of the lodges became redundant.)

Cross over and go up the signposted track opposite, point X, soon to reach point Y, the southern tip of Howe Wood. For an optional extension from this point see note at end. For the basic ramble turn sharp left along another track beside power poles, down to Brick House Farm.

Here turn left through the farmyard to a road (point Z). Do not enter the road but turn about to face the way you came and fork left onto a track then immediately turn left to a stile to the left of a gate. Cross and head diagonally across a meadow (with a house away to the right) to a gate in the far left-hand corner of the meadow. (The path is shown on maps to be on the far side of the house but as there is now a stile beside the gate the way described above appears to be now accepted as the route to follow.)

Turn left through a gate and keep along the right-hand branch of the track beyond. There will be a stream (the Debden Water) on your left.

After a narrow stretch another meadow is entered. Keep left beside the stream to the far end. Here get over a stile to the right of a gate and continue forward on a woodland path.

You come out of the wood on to a track called Bromley Lane and continue forward on it disregarding the right-hand branch. As it nears Newport its surface improves and you subsequently pass under a low railway viaduct.

Before this, the track joins a lane. Turn left along this for a few yards to the B1383. Again turn left over a bridge (a former toll bridge). Note, on the wall of a cottage, a former toll house, opposite, a list of tolls. A score of pigs and sheep would cost you a halfpenny but a single bull, or presumably, a much-married one, would cost fourpence.

You are now at the north end of the village and a stroll to the left will lead you back to the station with perhaps a stop on the way for refreshments.

Note: optional extension

At point Y continue forward just inside the wood. On my visit I found another track going just outside the wood but this may only be temporary. The track you should be on bends deeper into the wood. After going over a crosstrack, notice on the left an old milestone. So far as I have been able to check, there never was any highway here (2½ miles from Saffron Walden) and I can only presume that the stone was put there by a former owner of Debden Hall who may have contemplated turning this track into a private or turnpike road.

The track continues straight on beyond the wood with good views to the left and brings you to a lane elbow. Here turn rightwards and very soon bend squarely right. Follow the lane past farmhouses through Purton End for ¾ mile. At crossroads turn right for 500 yards. You will then re-reach point X and proceed along the track to point Y. Here turn left and continue with the main walk.

HENHAM, MOLE HALL AND AMBERDEN HALL

WALK 3

★

2½, 4½ or 6½ miles (4, 7 or 10.5 km)

OS Landranger 167

As will be noted from the sketch map, the full route of 6½ miles (based on Henham) can, by the use of the road link A–B, be turned into two shorter routes.

1. From Henham to point A and then (possibly after a slight detour to Mole Hall) along the lane link A–B to pick up the full route at point B. This option gives a circular, Henham-based walk of about 4½ miles.

2. Starting from the Mole Hall car park (near point A) follow the northern part of the main route round to point B then leave it and take the lane link B–A back to Mole Hall. This option — a circular walk based on Mole Hall — logs up about 2½ miles.

Mole Hall Wildlife Reserve houses a fine collection of native and foreign animals and birds. There is a car park, a picnic area, toilet facilities and a souvenir shop.

A worthwhile visit here would take quite two hours so those who like to combine a visit with a short walk may well prefer the third option I give and base the walk on Mole Hall.

Green lanes with their profusion of wild flowers in season feature much in this walk. These bridleways can be very muddy in winter so this walk is probably best done between late spring and early autumn. The route was explored for you in midwinter, however.

To Henham go along the M11 to its junction with the A120 (just east of Bishops Stortford). Here take the first exit at the roundabout to the B1383. At Stansted get on to the B1051 and follow it north-eastwards until a mile or so past Elsenham, you can turn leftwards (north) for Henham. (On approaching the village be careful to avoid the ducks which wander freely in the roads.) You pass the new school on your right and can shortly turn right onto a track beside the old school to turn left to park in the playground of the old school. After parking return to the road and continue ahead. At a T-junction turn right. The ponds from which the walk starts are seen on the left.

For Mole Hall directly, make for Widdington village by branching off the B1383 — the erstwhile A11 — about a mile south of Newport and, at Widdington, continuing on a minor road until just after passing Mole Hall Lane on the left you come to the entrance of the Nature Reserve (also on the left).

Park in the car park provided for visitors. There is a charge.

WALK 3

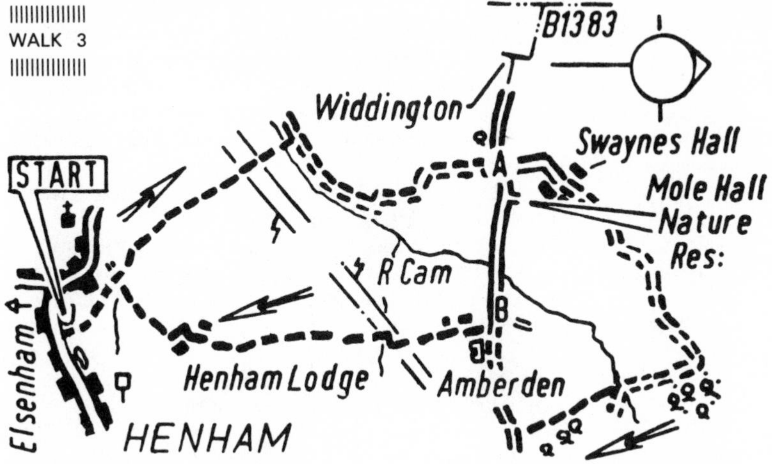

The Henham-based walks start in the high street at the end of a series of duck ponds with the Starr Garage opposite. *Face* the ponds and then go through a gate at their right-hand end and continue with a hedge on the left.

At the end of the field cross a bridge in a dip and follow the path left and right with a hedge and ditch on your left to a crossing drive. Continue over the drive, and on with a stream on your left. You soon pass a small lake or reservoir on your left and go ahead with a hedge on your right over a rise and under pylon lines to a field corner. Here, just beyond a pylon, cross to the other side of the hedge and continue your former direction through a gate and over a field to a stile and bridge over the stripling river Cam (by an electricity pole) into a hedged green lane.

Turn rightwards beside the river for ½ mile on a sometimes hedged and sometimes fenced lane. The lane is used by horseriders and there is a defined path to follow. The lane then turns squarely left away from the river and you follow the curvaceous way between hedges for a further mile to the road (point A).

For the full walk note that you now turn left and then, after 50 yards or so, take the right-hand Mole Hall Lane. Before doing this, however, you may wish to visit the wild life reserve. For this turn *rightwards* from point A for a short distance to the reserve entrance on the left.

For the shorter (4½ miles) walk turn rightwards from point A, soon passing the reserve entrance, and continue for about ¾ mile to the drive of Amberden Hall (point B) on the right and here rejoin the full walk where indicated in text.

Note that Widdington and its inn lies to the west (just turn leftwards at point A and keep on, ignoring the Mole Hall Lane turn). Return the same way. This detour adds about a mile each way however, and so portable drinks might be preferred. (Soft drinks and ice cream can be obtained at the reserve shop but there is no café.)

To continue with the main walk at point A turn left for about 50 yards and then go rightwards in Mole Hall Lane, bearing rightwards past Swaynes Hall and then left past the Mole Hall private entrance. You continue between old stables on the right (currently housing chickens) and a wall and fence on the left, then on a hedged green lane. You cross a gap and proceed along a further stretch of green lane with fine views leftwards over the valley towards Debden (see Walk 2) and then out into a field. Here turn half left on a track with a hedge on the left.

When the hedge on the left ends, go through a gap in a transverse hedge and on along a track over a field (slightly leftwards) towards a clump of trees. (This is, in reality, a further hedged section of the green lane.) Keep on for a further ½ mile and then turn rightwards on a track at the edge of a wood with the wood on your left and continue with the track beyond the wood. It later comes out into a more open section of track and after about 50 yards appears to enter a field ahead..

Here go half rightwards for about 10 yards with a hedge on your right then through a gap in a crossing hedge. Then turn left uphill towards a wood, with a hedge on your left. Pass the wood on your left and continue downhill to go through a gap in the hedge ahead at the bottom of the hill into a hedged green lane. Turn rightwards for ¼ mile, past a wide green lane on your left.

Soon, at Thistley Cottage (passed on your right) the track becomes made up. Very shortly after this (opposite Thistley Lodge on the right) turn left up the drive to Amberden Hall.

This is point B, where those taking the shorter walk rejoin the main route.

Pass a moat on your left and fork rightwards between farm buildings thus passing Amberden Hall on your left. Beyond farm buildings go ahead on a track with a hedge on your left. When the hedge ends, cross a bridge and go ahead uphill on a fine open track between crops with sweeping views as you proceed up and over a rise and under electricity lines. In a dip cross a bridge and follow the track with a leftward inclination uphill and later with a ditch on the left which you follow left and right beside the track towards Henham Lodge. Turn rightwards with the track in front of the lodge and then left through barns. At a T-junction turn left, still between barns, to a further T-junction at the end of the buildings. Here turn rightwards. Follow for a short ½ mile passing a track leading left and going downhill (with views over the lake passed on the outward route) into a dip by a stream. Here you rejoin the outward route and turn left with a ditch and hedge on your right as you follow the path ahead and then left to a bridge in a dip on the right. Cross and follow the hedge on your right back to the high street at Henham. Continue ahead over the road and green to the Starr Garage where you turn right and follow a lane and later a path past delightful thatched houses back to the old school which is on your right.

GREAT DUNMOW AND DUCK STREET

WALK 4

★

5 miles (8 km)

OS Landranger 167

Great Dunmow is a pleasant but apparently unexciting old market town which grew up at the point where the Roman Stane Street (now the A120) crossed the river Chelmer.

Everyone has heard of the Dunmow Flitch, however. This amusing prize was first given in the 13th century (thus making some present-day TV quizzes so very ancient) 'to any couple who will take oath in a prescribed manner that they have not quarrelled or repented of their marriage within a year and a day of its celebration'. After a mock trial, the winners were chaired around the town. The ceremony has been revived from time to time. It originated at Little Dunmow.

To reach Great Dunmow from London go by the M11 to Bishops Stortford. At the Start Hill exit leave to join the A120. Alternatives are to use the A113 to Chipping Ongar and then take the B184 via Leaden Roding; or (but this is longer) to take the A12 to Chelmsford and then take the A130 to Great Dunmow.

The car park in White Street, just off the High Street (behind the Boar's Head) is pay and display Mondays to Saturdays but free on Sundays and bank holidays.

From the car park turn rightwards into White Street and follow past Boyes Croft to emerge at the junction of main roads. Here turn rightwards into Market Place and then fork left down the narrow Star Lane, soon passing Doctor's Pond, and up to a crossing road.

Go ahead up a road which later has a belt of trees in the centre. Keep to the right of these trees and at the end of the road go ahead on a path between a house on the right and (at present) black sheds or barns on the left. This path runs on the left-hand side of a new housing estate and comes out to a junction. Ignore the path which continues to the right by some houses and turn *left* onto a hedged track. This soon turns right and continues to a field.

From here go diagonally across the field half left on a defined path to the opposite side by a wood. Go rightwards with a barbed wire fence on your left. You pass a gate on the left and about 50 yards beyond this the clear path swings left to go steeply downhill into a dip and over a stream. It then continues uphill bearing right and left to pass round the outside of a house and garden. Beyond the house continue on the track with a hedge on your left to emerge on a metalled drive beside a dutch barn. Turn right for a few yards along this past a house on your right. Just after this (and opposite an iron gate on your right) veer left on to a faint

WALK 4

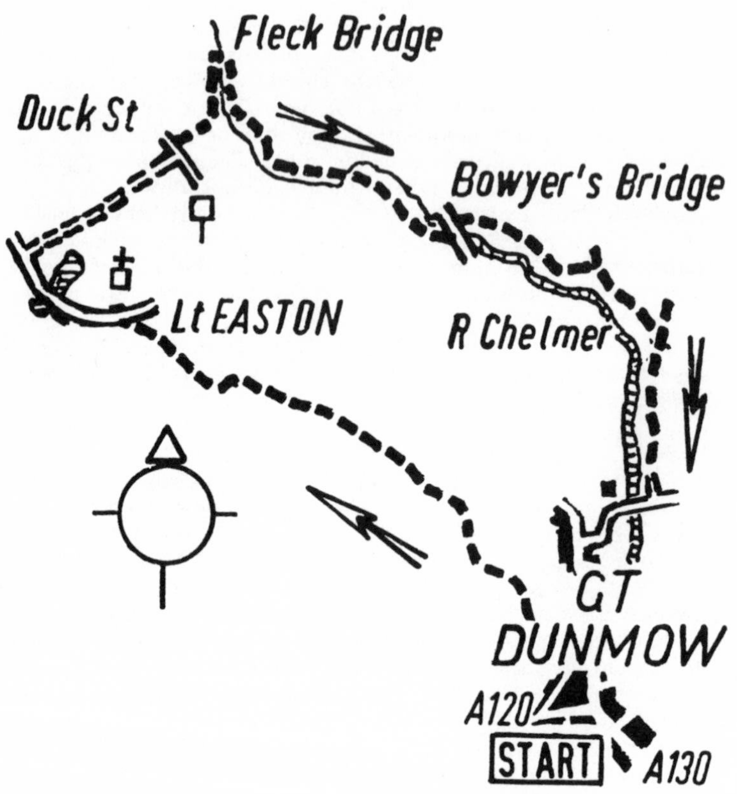

Fleck Bridge
Duck St
Bowyer's Bridge
Lt EASTON
R Chelmer
GT
DUNMOW
A120
START
A130

path across the grass into the corner and go leftwards through the gap. Follow the hedge on your right soon bending rightwards and by a clear path across a field through a gap and out to a road opposite the corner of the Little Easton churchyard.

Here turn left past the church to a junction with the rectory on your left and the Little Easton Manor on your right. Take the road ahead, downhill, to pass attractive ponds on either side and up to another junction near to a large house (Easton Glebe). Here turn rightwards along a track (a signposted public bridleway) at first with a wood on your right going gradually downhill and on to the corner of another wood. Carry on (passing a playing field on your left and houses) to a road opposite the Stag Inn.

Turn left and then right along the estate road (Butchers Pasture), as indicated by a public footpath sign, opposite the war memorial. When the road ends go forward down a rough field to a plank and stile. Cross this and follow an unploughed strip half-left across the next field to another plank bridge (with handrail) and on again for a few yards to a concrete footbridge over the river Chelmer.

Having crossed this, turn right and follow the many twists and turns of the river bank until you reach a stile. Cross this and veer rightwards and follow the river bank again, but now with a barbed wire fence on your left.

Eventually go through a field gate and on again, soon crossing an overflow channel and adjacent iron gate and field gates, which, as with others, you should take care to close.

Go through and shut the gate leading into the garden of Little Easton Mill and ahead with the mill on your right. At the corner of the mill turn right onto a path beside it and out through a gate to a road where the public footpath sign reassures you.

Turn left down the lane to the main B184 road and then left over a bridge for a few yards. Just before a cottage with pointed 'gothic' windows, turn rightwards through an iron gate and follow an unploughed grass track ahead until you reach a metalled road. Veer rightwards along this, and follow for some distance until you reach a path on your right leading over a narrow strip of field to a concrete footbridge. Cross this and (with the churchyard on your left) follow out to the church and Church Street.

Go forward along the road past the Angel and Harp and where the road turns right you go forward leftwards onto a track soon passing a house called Willow Bank and keeping to the right of the field gate bear right into open fields. Turn left with the hedge on your left. Continue along the left edge of a second field and in the corner with some houses ahead go leftwards through a hedge on your left and on along the right edge of the field with house gardens on your right. This leads into a fenced path between houses which you follow ahead. Cross a road and continue on the fenced path to its end at a junction with a road on your right. Turn right up the road and (opposite Blue Chip Associates on the right) turn left into the rear of the car park.

BRAINTREE AND BOCKING

WALK 5

★

5½ miles (9 km)

OS Landranger 167

Having completed a business visit to Braintree I thought I would stroll through its streets and the immediately surrounding fields. The following walkabout is typical of many you could get around many a thriving town where the old and the new combine.

What is generally referred to as present-day Braintree is, in fact, the combined neighbours-turned-brothers area of the old settlement of Braintree on the south side of the Roman road (the Stane Street, now the A120) and the old village of Bocking to its north. Another Roman road, the present-day A131 intersects and it is easy to see how the original settlement came into being.

In these days of racial integration, the case of the Flemish weavers, fleeing the Huguenot persecution, has often been cited. They brought their skills and thus prosperity to such places as Braintree.

To the north of the 16th century Dorewards Hall is a prominent post mill of *c.* 1680, moved to its present position in 1830 — a pleasant sight to compensate for the inevitable latter-day buildings in an area where you cannot expect deep rurality.

To Braintree from London take the M11 to the Start Hill roundabout, just east of Bishops Stortford, and then take the A120 via Great Dunmow. Or take the A12 to Chelmsford, followed by the A130 northwards to Little Waltham and then by the A131.

There is a car park adjoining the railway station (long stay) and another (main one) in Fairfield Road. There is another coyly hidden away in the unnamed road on the west side of the RC Church of Our Lady Queen of Peace. The three car parks are, as will be seen, on the direct line of the ramble route.

If starting from the station car park go leftwards to the Railway pub. Here turn left and then, at the police station, rightwards up Fairfield Road.

If starting from the Fairfield Road car park join the walk here.

Continue to the top of the road passing the late 1920s town hall on the way. So you reach the Nag's Head on your right. Keeping right to pass Cramphorn's corner shop, turn right along a narrow unnamed street, past another car park on your left.

Those using this third option car park join the walk here.

Continue to the RC Church of Our Lady Queen of Peace which stands on the corner of The Avenue. Now continue forward along a passageway, over a transverse road and on to emerge on to Manor Street by crossroads at the 'International'. Go forward for 250 yards until you

WALK 5

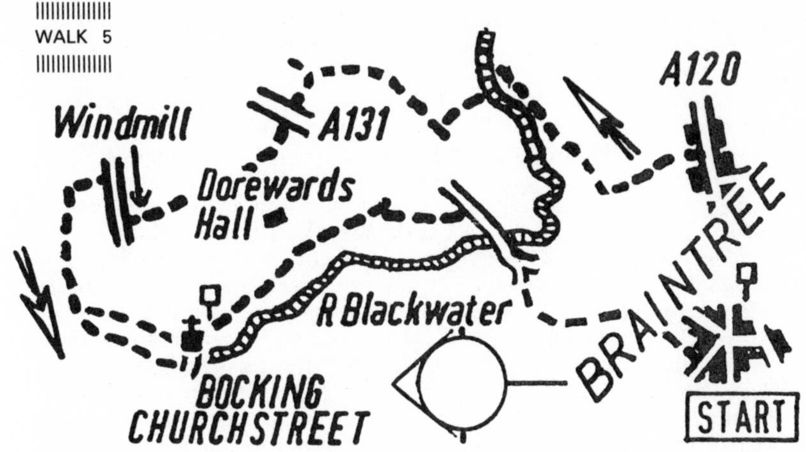

reach the second left turn (East Street) at Lake & Elliot's Sports & Social Club. Turn left to the Eagle and A120. Turn right crossing with care to turn left beside house no 125 on a path leading down the side of a sports field. When this reaches the end of a little road turn right through railings and immediately left down a concrete backway behind houses until you reach a field. Here veer rightwards gradually descending and subsequently taking a leftward fork away from the hedge to turn left to cross three little bridges over the river Blackwater at the site of Strait's Mill.

After crossing these, turn left along a rough gravel track and ignoring a track leading to the right into gravel workings, continue ahead on a concrete track with the river to your left. Some 75 yards after joining concrete track and after passing three power poles turn right through a layby (opposite a track leading left to the river) and continue uphill with a hedge on the right. Go over a transverse track and continue uphill with a hedge and deep water on right. Where the track turns left with scrub on the right turn left for 25 yards then right on a hidden path. (If you continue to where the track bears right you have gone too far.) After 5 yards reach and turn right on a sunken hedged lane. These delightful unmade green lanes which were the original cart roads of Essex are a wonderful haven for birds and wild flowers.

The sunken green lane leads uphill with gravel workings behind a hedge on the right and on reaching another path fork left out to Thistly Green Road at bungalows where you turn left to the A131 road. Cross straight over and take the forward signposted path which gradually veers rightwards with Dorewards Hall away to your left and continues along a power line towards the windmill, and eventually between houses out to a road. Turn right along this, past a cul de sac on the left and after 150 yards turn left (opposite house no 254) on a signposted footpath towards a barn. This leads downhill to a footbridge over a stream. Cross and immediately turn left over a field with the stream on your left. Turn right over second stile on the right and turn left with a hedge on the left to reach a road by way of a gap in the hedge in the field corner.

Turn left along the road, and round a bend to a signposted path on your right. Immediately inside the field turn left on a wide track with a fence on the left to Bocking Hall. At the end of the track where you reach a fence you will find there are two stiles by which to cross the fence (rather a his and hers situation). Beware the stile on the right which is rather frail. Continue on a fenced path (with the hall on the right) and turn left with the path past a delightful pond and on over a stile onto a drive. Follow this ahead alongside the churchyard wall to a road opposite The Retreat. Turn right and left past the ornate parish hall and turn right over a road junction to enter a wide track to the right of almshouses beside a Bovingdon road sign. On the right over the open space where Courtaulds once stood but has now been demolished there is an impressive view of Bocking church. After crossing the river turn left with a Courtaulds building on your left, out to a road opposite a distinctive black and white house by Bocking waterworks. Turn left across the river again and right along Dorewards Avenue. When this turns left go forward along a metalled track.

Where the metalled track turns left go ahead on a path between crops with a power line slightly to your right. At the hedge corner on the right, the path should go half right across the field following the line of power poles to join a hedge corner and continue with the hedge on the left. It now however seems common practice to continue ahead beside the hedge slightly uphill to the field corner and turn right with the hedge on your left to rejoin the path by turning left in the corner with the hedge on the left.

Continue beside the hedge and in the next corner bear leftwards to a wicket gate leading out to the A131 by the convent. Turn rightwards on the road noting the coats of arms on the bridge. The road is known progressively, as Convent Hill, Broad Road and Bradford Street and soon passes the ex-Tudor House Museum.

Continue ahead, ignoring on your right the B1053 and later Woolpack Lane until you reach the King's Head. Opposite this turn right along Friars Lane. When this ends cross a stile and go half left across a field and over a stile into a new housing estate. Turn right onto a road to a T-junction where you turn left and beside house no 29 turn right over rough grass to join a rough road leading ahead. Go forward along this for some distance until you reach St Peter's in the Field church. Continue ahead along St Peter's Walk to another road where you then turn left to the main road and left again to the White Hart Hotel.

Here turn sharp right along Bank Street with Lloyds Bank on the corner to The Swan, left along Swan Lane and right down an alley leading to Leather Lane. Then on to a further road opposite the Halifax Building Society's premises and finally left back to the market square.

BUSH END GATE AND HATFIELD FOREST

WALK 6

★

5½ miles (9 km)

OS Landranger 167

The Forest of Hatfield (not to be confused with the Hertfordshire Hatfield) is an old deer park which once formed part of the estates of the Houblons of Hallingbury Place. It is all that remains of a once extensive Royal Hunting Ground — part of the great Forest of Essex.

In the early 1920s the Hallingbury Estate was broken up and concern was expressed at the felling of a great number of fine trees. Thanks to the generosity of the Buxton family and later benefactors the forest was saved and presented to the National Trust. It now comprises over a thousand acres of woodland: fewer large trees than of yore but with coppices of oak and hornbeam and many fine maples with scattered stands of silver birch. Armed with a pocket-size book on tree identification, the visitor will find specimens of many other of our native trees: alder, black poplar, elm, horse chestnut, etc, and much thorn (often sporting a mistletoe bough).

Needless to say, there is a wealth of flora and fauna. A nature trail, starting from the Shell House, has been laid out. A guide to the trail may be bought.

The forest is intersected by many rides and drives which have intriguing names, some of which I have given for their old-world charm. The wide grassy 'vista' which bisects the forest north to south is named 'London Road' and was, at one time, exactly this. The proximity of Stansted airport makes the area less quiet than it once was.

Drive up the M11 to its junction with the A120 just east of Bishops Stortford. Now go in the Great Dunmow direction for 2 miles (you are on the course of the ancient Stane Street) and towards the end of the village of Takeley Street (not to be confused with Takeley itself farther along the road) turn rightwards (nearly opposite the Green Man) on a road signposted to Hatfield Forest. In ½ mile or so a right-hand signpost directs you into a car park. A charge of £2.00 is made during the summer season (not Thursdays) but this goes towards the upkeep of the forest. If you visit the forest on Thursdays however the refreshment building is closed.

From the top end of the car park, enter the forest through a gate and follow a metalled track ahead round bends. About 25 yards before this metalled track enters a belt of woodland (Elgin Coppice) fork half left on a concrete path and on between two belts of woodland to where two gates are visible in fencing ahead. Turn left through the left-hand gate

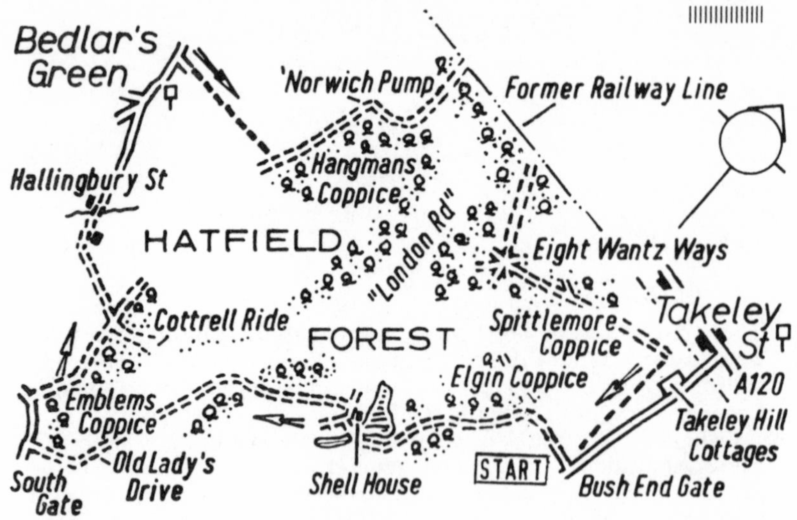

by a notice that reads 'No fishing please on this side of the lake' and go ahead with a large lake soon visible on your right.

Keep ahead beside the lake on an earthen dam called (an example of bucolic wit probably going back to the early immigration days) 'America'. This leads on over a causeway which separates the main lake from its narrower arm and to the recreation area in front of the Shell (or Grotto) House — a charming example of the architectural conceits with which many 18th century landowners liked to embellish their grounds. Embedded in its walls are shells, flints, clinkers and pieces of glass. Above the door a falcon (?) with outstretched wings, fashioned from oyster shells, will be noticed.

Here will be found conveniences, benches, a shelter and, at propitious times, refreshments.

Walk beside the lake with the Shell House on your left then turn left past the refreshment building to a gate leading over a tarmac track. Go straight on over an open grassy area slightly right to the right-hand edge of woodland and on, soon passing a tall cedar tree on your right. Bear left over a bridge through a gap between woods onto a long wide ride. This comes out onto an even wider transverse ride, part of the London Road mentioned in my introductory remarks but here called Old Lady's Drive. As you turn left down this ride the white walled Forest Lodge can be seen through gaps on your right. Continue on along this ride until a boundary fence limits your way ahead. Here turn rightwards by the fence, soon coming to the South Gate. Do *not* go through this out to the lane. Instead continue inside the boundary into a wood, Emblems Coppice, to a corner. Ignore, here, a left-hand stile which gives exit to the lane. Instead turn *squarely right*, on a wide grassy track just inside the woodland edge.

After about ½ mile you reach a white gate on the left with a ride (Cotterell) to the right. Go leftwards through this gate, ignoring a right-hand fork into stables, and ahead on an enclosed track. This might be somewhat soft in parts after a spell of rainy weather but it presently becomes 'made' and runs into a lane elbow. Here you continue forward to reach the Hop Poles at Bedlar's Green — about 3 miles from the start.

In front of the inn turn rightwards. There is soon a triple fork in front of the village post office. Take the left-hand branch (signposted as a public footpath). Very shortly fork right on a path with a hedge and ditch on your right.

So you reach the forest perimeter track. The diversion I have just given (mostly lane walking) was to enable those who require it to reach an inn.

Turn left in this perimeter track with a wood, Hangman's Coppice, on your right. In ¼ mile (at a corner most intriguingly marked on larger scale maps as 'Norwich Pump' — another bit of old-time bucolic wit?) turn right and soon left, still skirting the wood.

Cross a stile and continue ahead leftish on a grassy track which eventually leads out into a grassy area. Turn right to the left-hand edge of a belt of woodland which is on the far side of the green to your right and turn left onto a track leading through a gate onto the dismantled railway. This is now a linear country park between Bishops Stortford and Braintree (a distance of some 15 miles) and is delightful to walk at some future date when time permits. Details available from 'Ways through Essex' who are based at the Essex County Council offices in Chelmsford. After ¼ mile turn right over a stile by a gate and follow a wide straight ride through the forest to a junction of eight tracks named Eight Wantz (Wantz meaning Ways). Turn left on a wide ditched horse ride walking on the grassy path beside it (Spittlemore Ride) ignoring a left fork. After going over a transverse track the way narrows a bit. Cross a stile into a large grassy area with ahead to the left the modern Takeley Hill Cottage (the quarters of the forest's head ranger).

Turn right keeping between the woodland on the right and the lane which runs parallel on your left passing a cottage on your left. The grass is tufty but there are a number of well-defined paths which can be followed leading you on to cross a stile in the right-hand side of a transverse fence. You cross the drive leading from the now stopped up Halfway Gate and bear half left to a stile leading into the bottom of the car park.

CHAPPEL AND EARLS COLNE

WALK 7

★

7½ miles (12 km) or 6 miles (9.3 km)

OS Landranger 168

A walk over low hills with fine views, passing a watermill and Chalkney wood before returning via a reservoir for possible refreshments at the Swann Inn in Chappel with its riverside garden. A chance to explore the delights of the Colne Valley.

Chappel is on the A604 between Halstead and Colchester and also on the railway between Marks Tey and Bures. Parking is usually available at the station where time should be taken to visit the railway museum. There is also a refreshment room at the station and the museum has working engines and organises steam days throughout the summer.

From the station return to the road and turn right uphill. Take the first road on the right (Spring Gardens Road) soon crossing the railway. Here turn left by the footpath signpost and follow a hedge on the left. In the corner go ahead through a gap and on with the hedge on your left to a wood. Enter the wood by a path about 5 yards from the corner on a narrow path which turns right to run along the edge of the wood and up a bank to turn left onto a broader path. At the end of the wood, where the path turns right, turn left on a narrow path to and over the level crossing.

On the far side ignore the gate and being careful of a drop on the left, turn right and left to cross a plank bridge and go straight on across a field aiming for a gap to the left of a bungalow and an electricity pole and so out to a road. (Willow Cottage is up the road to your right.) Cross to a footpath opposite and at the end of a garden on the right turn right for about 10 yards. Then opposite the garden gate turn left on a track aiming for the hedge corner and carry on with the hedge on your right.

At a field corner cross the earth bridge and continue ahead aiming for the right-hand edge of the hedge line by an electricity pole. Cross a stile and continue ahead with the hedge on the left to a road. Turn right, climbing gently uphill, and at a junction keep ahead leftish. Beyond a green with a stone seat on your left, turn left (signposted White Colne). You pass the delightfully named June Cottage on your right and at Home Farm on the left where the road bears right go ahead on the drive to Norman Farm.

Where the drive goes into the farm continue through the gate ahead with the hedge on your left steeply downhill into the field corner. Cross a stile and continue ahead between the fence on the right and the wood on the left. Cross a bridge and go ahead over a narrow field with a hedge on the right. In the corner turn left with a hedge curving on your right.

WALK 7

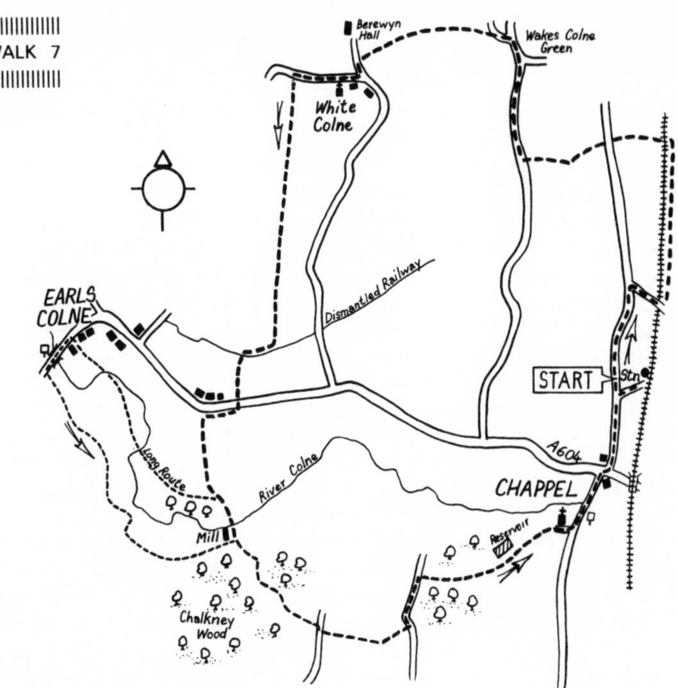

There are delightful views to the left. When the tall trees on the right end (about 30 yards short of farm buildings) turn right by the waymark (on top of a post) and ahead with a hedge on your left.

Cross a stile and with care a narrow ditch and drive, to continue on a hedged green lane to a road. Turn right past a church with welcoming seats in the churchyard and 25 yards short of the road junction ahead turn left on a signposted footpath following the line of trees on your left. At the end of some trees bear left and right and continue your forward direction on a track. At a crossing hedge go over a bridge and continue on the track to a distant crossing hedge in the valley. Turn right beside the hedge and the now dismantled railway line. At a gap turn left over the track and right with the dismantled railway now on your right. After about 100 yards you come to a waymark in the hedge (opposite a garage on the road on your left) and turn left to reach the road by a footpath sign. Cross with care and turn right then a little further on turn left onto a little lane called Chalkney Mill Lane and follow to where a pylon line crosses the lane.

Here you have a choice of a longer walk to Earls Colne for refreshments and a view of the priory or of continuing ahead on the short walk past the mill. For the short walk, beyond the mill continue ahead through double gates onto a track by a notice about sporting woods and continue from (**X**) below.

For the long walk turn right by the pylon over the stile beside the gate. Follow waymarks to turn right, with a lake on your right, bearing right to a bridge and stile. Continue with a hedge on your right and when it turns right turn half right uphill on an obvious path to join the river Colne coming in from the left. Keep ahead beside the river over stiles and through a gate to the main road at Earls Colne where you turn left and over a bridge across the river Colne.

Beyond the bridge you can either continue ahead to the Coachman Inn (which is almost opposite the priory) for refreshments and a chance to explore Earls Colne then retrace your steps or continue with the walk by turning left shortly after the bridge on a footpath to the right of house No. 32 (leading to No. 34). Keep ahead beside a fence on the right to a gate. Continue over stiles and through gates beside a hedge until you come to a collection of gates. Here look out for a stile on your right. Cross and turn left with the hedge now on your left (ie change side of hedge). If an electric fence is still in the field go through the gate at its left-hand edge, otherwise keep ahead to the field corner where you turn right for about 20 yards to cross a fence on the left over a bridge onto a track (at the point where the fence ends). Cross the track to a rusted-up iron gate (it may be easier to use the field gates on your left to bypass the rusted-up iron gate) and go ahead with the hedge on your left passing under a pylon line. At the end of the field cross a stile and go ahead with the hedge on your left. Cross a stile and follow the fence between mill buildings to the lane. Here turn right through the double gates between buildings onto a track and past the notice about sporting woods and the need to keep dogs on leads.

(**X**) Continue ahead on the track into the wood going gently uphill. Towards the top of the rise fork left (ignoring waymarks for the 'Wildside Walk' pointing right). Ignore the track on the right and at the end of the wood go through gates along a hedged path to a lane. Cross to a footpath almost opposite and follow a green lane to a stile and bridge into a field. Go ahead steeply uphill with outstanding views behind (and if you are lucky, flights of Canada geese) to a stile in the fence at the corner. Cross and go ahead with the fence on your left and reservoir on your right. Beyond here the path should continue ahead but it is blocked by blackcurrant bushes so turn left, skirting round the edge of the plantation.

Bear round to the right with the bushes and at their end, at a wood corner, turn left into the wood on a track. At the point where the track bears left at the end of the wood on the left be very careful to *fork half right* on a narrow path on the *left edge* of a wood. Cross a stile erected by the Colchester group of the Ramblers Association and turn right with the wood on your right. Cross a stile and bridge and continue between the wood on your right and the new reservoir on your left.

At the wood corner turn right for 10 yards then left beside a fence. In the next corner cross a bridge and stile on the right and turn left by a waymark on a short track to turn right over a stile and follow a hedge on the left.

Cross stiles with the hedge on the left and later on the right alongside grassy meadows to pass the church on the left and so reach the road at Chappel. Turn left past the Swann Inn, and at a crossroads on the A604 with a shop on the right, continue ahead to the station and car.

AYTHORPE RODING, WOOLARDS ASH AND HELLMANS CROSS

WALK 8

★

5 miles (8 km)

OS Landranger 167

The Rodings (or 'Roothings'), of which there are eight — Abbess, Aythorpe, Beauchamp, Berners, High, Leaden, Margaret, and White — take their name from the river Roding, and are mostly tiny and scattered places, their ancient churches often standing lonely amid the cornfields. That at Aythorpe Roding from which we start stands on a narrow farm road.

Essex may not have high hills but it has a charm of its own in the quiet, secluded river valleys and the rolling countryside such as is found on this present walk.

To Aythorpe Roding take the A113 through Wanstead and Abridge to Ongar, where you continue ahead on the B184 via Fyfield to meet the transverse B1060. Here turn rightwards to join the B184 again at Leaden Roding. Here turn left (northwards). After nearly a mile note over to your left a restored windmill; another of those maintained by the Essex County Council (cf. that of Stock on Walk 30). Continue along the road soon to reach a crossroad at the Axe and Compasses. Here turn left for ½ mile looking carefully for a narrow lane on the left leading to the church of Aythorpe Roding. Turn in here.

Park discreetly by the church.

After parking, retrace your way from the church to the T-junction and here turn left downhill. In ¼ mile or so, after disregarding a public bridleway sign on the right, and immediately after crossing a stream — the Roding — turn rightwards on the Newhall drive (signposted as a public footpath).

After ½ mile you pass the farm buildings (going round a square left-hand bend).

Continue your way, now on a green track with a hedge on the right, for another ¼ mile to a stream with an earth bridge. Do *not* cross. Instead, turn left with a hedge on the right. At the end of the field get over a ditch and enter a green lane, turning right and left with the lane. After about 300 yards turn squarely rightwards with the track. After ¼ mile or so it makes a quick right-left bend and becomes surfaced.

Follow this quiet lane uphill with fine views and past houses with nice gardens. The erstwhile square left-right bend at Woolards Ash has now been bypassed by a new bit of road so that you pass Woolards Ash on your left. Keep on the road for a further short ½ mile and a couple of

WALK 8

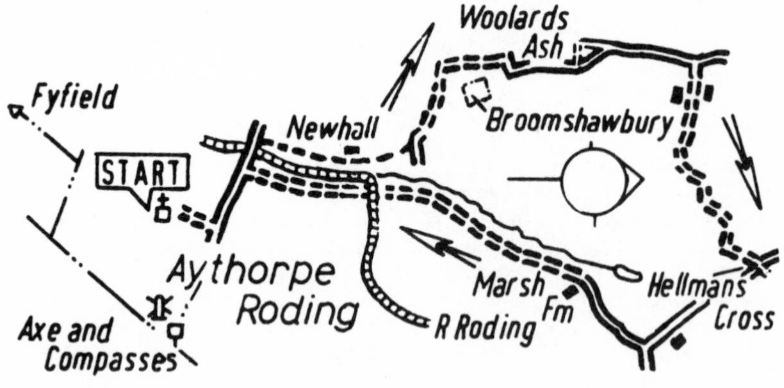

hundred yards after passing a green lane on the left turn rightwards on a track, soon passing Aldbury's Farm on the right. For the first ⅜ mile the track is a straight one, but afterwards it bends left and becomes quite curvaceous and very lovely. In a mile or so from Aldbury's you reach a road at Hellmans Cross.

Turn rightwards in the lane, ignore the first right-hand offshoot you come to but, just over ½ mile from Hellmans Cross and where the lane turns sharply left, turn rightwards on a minor road which, in ¼ mile, becomes the drive of Marsh Farm.

Keep to the right of the farm buildings and where the made-up drive ends continue forward to enter a green lane. This is — or was when the survey for this book was being made — a little overgrown in places but it is hopefully due for clearance and the way might be quite clear by the time this book is published and you come this way. The track has a fence on its right and runs out into a field. Keep ahead (right) with a hedge on the right for about ½ mile. The footpath-like section then reverts to a short section of green lane and brings you out to a bridge over the infant river Roding.

Continue ahead with a hedge on the left and a view of Aythorpe Roding church ahead. Then maintain your direction over a field and on, with a hedge on your right, over ditches and, lastly, veering right into a green lane leading ahead to a road. Here turn left and then rightward, back to Aythorpe Roding church.

PLESHEY, NORTH END AND BLACKCHAPEL

WALK 9

★

7 miles (11 km)

OS Landranger 167

Pleshey is a moated village with some fine houses and a small green area with seats overlooking the moat and castle mound. The castle is no longer open (except by appointment) but can be viewed from the outside from the footpath on the right of the main road in Pleshey (just beyond the White Horse pub) or from the charming recreation area in the main road (opposite the Leather Bottle pub) where there are seats and a view of the castle and its moat with ducks. Little of the masonry of the castle remains except a lofty, pointed, brick arch which spans the moat and connects the keep-mound with the castle yard. The earthworks however are impressive; the keep-mound being slightly oval in shape, 900 ft in circumference and rising 50 ft above its moat. It is probably of Saxon origin. We follow good tracks to the hamlet of North End with its delightful houses and the 15th century Blackchapel named after the Augustinian Canons who wore black cloaks. It is entirely timber framed with a priest house attached and is open daily from 9.30 to 5.30 except Monday and Tuesday. There is a note on its history on the wall. (If visiting please scrape off and leave outside any mud collected on shoes on the walk.) A feature of the walk is the fine Essex scenery with its wide open skies and low rolling hills.

To Pleshey take the A113 from Wanstead to Ongar and on over the Four Wantz (or ways) roundabout to Fyfield. Pass a turning to Willingale in the village by the Queens Head and pass the Black Bull on the right. Turn right at the next turning. Beyond here be careful. The ride is charming but Essex lanes can be narrow and winding and there is always the chance of a farm vehicle beyond the bend, particularly in spring and around harvest time. Follow up to a T-junction with a private house (the erstwhile Two Swans) ahead. Turn right and then left for Margaret Roding. Follow to a T-junction with the main road. Turn right for just over ½ mile and by the Fountain Inn on the left turn left for the Easters. This road has a couple of sharp bends and a very narrow bridge. Go over unmarked crossroads in Good Easter, and on to a T-junction. Turn right on a rather narrow road to a T-junction and turn left. Take the next road on your right, signposted Pleshey, passing the church on your right as you enter the village.

Park discreetly in the village.

The walk starts from the west end of the village by the church and new village hall. You may start either by walking round the moat (a) or through the village (b).

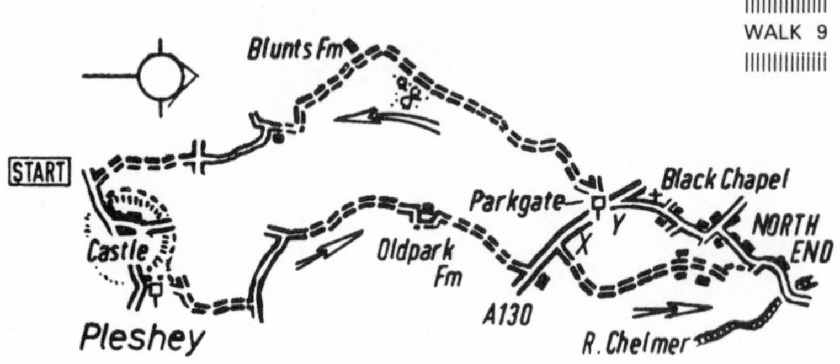

(a) Walk the footpath round the moat by taking the signposted path on the left just before the buildings start. Keep ahead bearing rightwards with the moat on your right. Go through a hedge gap and continue to a road. Cross and keep ahead with the moat on your right. At a hedge corner turn left with a hedge on the right and at the end of the hedge turn right into an open area. Follow a path over a slightly marshy area to a road. Turn about and head diagonally over the rough area (away from the road) to a bridge halfway along the hedge.

(b) Walk along the main road past the recreation area described above and at the end of the village (just beyond the end of a wall on the right) by a junction of two footpath signs on the right and also by entrance gates on the right turn left over a stile and head diagonally over a field to a stile and bridge halfway along the hedge on your right.

Continue along a path with newly planted trees to a hedge where you then turn left with a hedge on the right.

At the end of the hedge you come to, and turn rightwards in, a hedged track. Ignore, soon, a narrow track going off rightwards. Just after this go through a gap ahead and turn squarely left on a wide track hedged on its left. Follow it out to a road where a public bridleway sign confirms your right of way.

Turn left past Park Farm and where, just over ¼ mile farther on, the road bends sharply left, continue ahead (slightly rightwards) on a concreted track. There is a pedestrian and bridle right of way along it. The 'Private' notice on the right refers ambiguously to the adjacent fields and the fact that the track is not a public way for vehicles.

You go between fields, walking on the grass verge if you wish. On coming to a concrete area keep ahead on the right-hand track (hedge on right) *not* the left fork. On the outskirts of Old Park Farm you pass a pond on your right and then go squarely right and then squarely left round the farm. You then pass a pond on the left. Disregard, now, the left-hand track. Keep straight on, downhill through a gate.

The continuing track runs through a valley, fence on the left, and soon to an open meadow on the right. It later goes over a stream in a dip and, passing a bungalow on the right, brings you out to the A130 opposite Kings Farm.

Turn left for about 300 yards to a spot just beyond the end of the right-hand hedge and in front of a single oak tree (point X). *For the main ramble route turn rightwards* although note that, for a short cut, one may reach the Butcher's Arms by continuing along the road for a further ¼ mile.

For the footpath way (preferred) turn as just mentioned rightwards on the track. Go downhill, later with a hedge and orchard on the right. At the end of the orchard turn left on a track (away from the orchard) over a rise and across open fields towards buildings.

On coming to the buildings pass old cars and keep ahead into the yard and then straight on between buildings. At the end of these keep ahead past a pond on the left. At a track junction with houses ahead, turn rightwards. The track passes buildings on the right and goes ahead as a green lane (a little concealed at first) running slightly left of the track leading into a farmyard. After 350 yards or so turn left over a bridge. Here the way should continue as a green lane but seems to have been ploughed out. At this point the custom of those coming this way appears to be to turn left, following the hedge left and right towards houses seen ahead, and then turning rightwards towards the end of these houses. Finally turn leftwards on the remains of a green lane and so out to a road where mockingly, there is a public bridleway sign.

Turn left (you are now in the hamlet of North End) past Murrills with its pond on the left. At a junction turn left (for Great Waltham and Chelmsford) passing a track on the left and Brook House on the right where the lane turns rightwards over a stream and past Baytree Cottage. Beyond the houses the road has a grass verge and on the right you pass the 15th century timber-framed Blackchapel.

On joining the A130 turn left to the Butcher's Arms, now in view (point Y). From the right-hand side of the inn (as you face it) take the 'No Through Road'. There are some imposing houses on its right.

In 150 yards or so, just past 'Parkgate' disregard the footpath signpost pointing ahead. Instead, turn left on a concreted track. Beyond a concreted bay 300 yards on, the track turns rightwards and becomes grassy, hedged sometimes on both sides and sometimes on one or the other side. About ¼ mile farther on, the track curves gently leftwards. A little farther on there is an almost square right bend at the entrance to a field ahead. This bend, conspicuous on a map, is not at all obvious on the ground so take care here.

The track now rises and is concreted for a short distance. Ignore concreted side paths to left and right. The track becomes grassy again and subsequently passes a conifer wood on the left at the end of which you come to a concreted crossing track. Here turn right for only a few yards and then left on a concrete track towards Blunts Farm. Here be careful to keep *ahead* on the left edge of a concrete area passing the farm building on your right and large new barns on the left. Do NOT take the eye-catching concrete track that strikes off rightwards in front of the farm.

Follow this fine bridleway which winds and then goes round square bends and becomes more made up as it passes houses on the left and reaches a road elbow. Here go leftwards and follow to a transverse road. Take the hedged green lane opposite and follow it out to a road in which turn left, soon to reach Pleshey church.

MATCHING GREEN, COBBLER'S PIECES AND BLACKCAT

WALK 10

★

4½ or 8 miles (7 or 13 km)

OS Landranger 167

On this walk you may have a chance to watch cricket on the village green and there is the chance of a bit of luck at the quaintly named hamlet of Blackcat. The walk includes some nice tracks and houses and fine open views with spring and early summer flowers. The main walk admittedly crosses a few cropped fields but as the paths are fairly well used they become, hopefully, restored by use after ploughing.

To Matching Green take the A113 from Wanstead via Abridge to Ongar. Keep ahead over the Four Wantz (or ways) roundabout and shortly turn left for Moreton. (Moreton is consistently one of the best kept villages in Essex and is beautifully decorated with window boxes in spring and summer.) Enter Moreton, turn right over the bridge WITH CARE into the village and to a T-junction. Turn left, soon turning right with the road and following the signposted route north to Matching Green. Essex lanes can be beautiful but they are winding and narrow so please drive with care especially on bends. At the T-junction in Matching Green take care where turning right into the village as it is a blind corner with very poor visibility to the right.

Park discreetly in the village. (Subject to weather conditions parking is allowed on the green but ONLY on the edge beside the road.)

The walk starts from The Chequers at Matching Green. Pass this on your right with the green and its cricket pitch on your left. At the T-junction turn rightwards with Green Edge Cottages and the school sign on your left. Soon fork left (for Little Laver) and follow this for ¼ mile or so, round bends. Where it turns sharply right keep ahead on a concrete track towards an electricity pole. Follow the concrete track to the point where it turns sharp left. Here continue your line alongside a field edge with a ditch on your right towards a wood. Pass the north edge of the wood (ie keep the wood to your right).

At the hedge at the end of the field enter through a narrow gap to emerge after 10 yards into another field. Continue your line across this field, aiming just left of a short metal communications tower. At the hedge you join a concrete track where you turn right for a few yards until you are beyond the tower, and a trodden gap through the hedge becomes obvious. The gap leads to a good headland path in the next field running alongside a second wood (on your right).

Once into the second field follow the wood round to the right. This

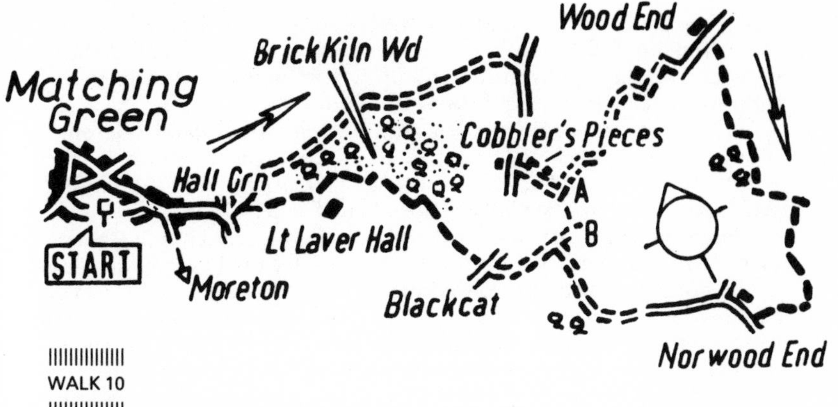

gradually curves left to resume your original line of direction. Proceed to the very end of the wood (very narrow at this point) then continue across a field aiming towards the right-hand of two distant houses, more or less straight ahead.

At the point where you draw level with a black water tower (when it is directly on your left-hand side) bear half right to join a ditch at a right angle corner. Cross the ditch at this point and continue with it on your left until it joins a lane at a public bridleway sign.

Note: If you are not agile enough to jump the ditch just continue (as so many people seem to do) with the ditch on your right and cross it at a corner where the path runs into the road.

From the public bridleway sign turn rightwards past Cobblers Cottages on the left (once derelict but now beautifully restored as Cobblers House).

In just over ½ mile from your point of entry to the road you come to a small group of buildings; farm buildings on the right and the quaintly named Cobbler's Pieces on the left. Note the fine 'herring-bone' barn on the left.

Immediately past Cobbler's Pieces turn left on a byway past 'Leaders' with its pretty garden. You soon come to a square left bend (point A). *For the shorter route* see note at end.

For the full round the next section is mostly easy trackways, with a (possibly) short section over cropped (but still walked) and easily negotiated fields. At point A, therefore, turn squarely left and follow round bends, sometimes as an open track and sometimes hedged on one side or the other.

There are fine views along this stretch, firstly with glimpses of the white spire of Abbess Roding church about a mile away to the north east (half left), then later (half right) with views of the lonely tower of Beauchamp (pronounced Beecham) Roding church. This becomes more of a dominant feature later. Eventually the track becomes a metalled lane and isolated houses are passed.

After about ¾ mile from point A you pass a thatched cottage on the left. About 200 yards beyond this turn right at a public footpath sign by some barns. Go straight across the field in the direction indicated by the sign. The path should, under the Agricultural Bill, be defined but failing this aim for the left-hand corner of a distant wood ahead. A ditch is crossed on the way by means of a plank bridge about 40 yards to the right of the electricity pole nearest to the ditch.

On gaining the wood proceed ahead along its left-hand side on a pleasant grassy track. (If the sun is in the right direction in the afternoon) you should be able to pick out, half left, the twin churches of Willingale Spain and Willingale Doe about 2 miles distant.

Soon after (on a clear day) the tower of High Easter church (some 5 miles distant) becomes visible away to the north east above and just left of the houses of Beauchamp Roding. At the end of the wood turn left along a track, soon crossing to the right-hand side of the hedge. In 300 yards turn rightwards on the right-hand side of the hedge. At the end of the hedge, cross a ditch and turn left with the ditch (or streamlet) on your left. In a further 250 yards, at a corner, leave the streamlet, turn right alongside another ditch and up a rise to reach a moat. Turn right (moat on left) and continue to a gate on the left. Turn left beside a hedge to a lane at Norwood End.

Turn rightwards in the delightful lane passing, in the garden of a house on your left, an old signpost pointing the way to Brentwood. In a short ¼ mile you come to a fork and ignore the right-hand branch to Hales Farm. Keep on past Lee Farm after which the lane becomes even more rural and eventually reverts to a hedged green lane and at a woodland corner bends rightwards then keeps straight on (north) until a leftward T-junction brings you out to the tiny hamlet of Blackcat.

Here those taking the short route join in. Cross to continue along the right-hand side of a builder's yard opposite and go left behind it to the outside of a hedge then go ahead with the hedge on your left. From the end of the garden on your left the path should be defined diagonally across the field to a gap about 20 yards short of an oak in the hedge. In the past, as is so often the case when the field is in crop, walkers appear to have taken a 'round the edge of the field' route to reach this hedge gap. Cross to the other side of the hedge and continue with hedge on the right towards a wood.

Continue ahead with the wood on your right then at the wood corner bear left for 20 yards. Here turn right through the bushes on a worn path across a ditch and into the next field where you continue half left aiming for a stile at the left-hand edge of another wood.

Cross the stile and proceed with the wood on your right and a house away to your left (Little Laver Hall) and on over two further stiles to turn left on a track through the trees.

At the end of a garden and tennis courts turn rightwards just before a gate on a short, well-defined path through a neck of woodland.

The path now runs diagonally over a large field to rejoin the concrete track by which we left Matching Green and is usually well kept and defined when the field is in crop. (However if you are unlucky enough to arrive when the path is not visible it may be easier to turn right beside the wood and in the corner cross the ditch ahead. Then turn left beside the ditch to rejoin the concrete track.) Here continue on the track to retrace a little of the outward route back to your car.

Note: *Cobbler's Pieces — Blackcat link for shorter walk.* At point A (where the track from Cobbler's Pieces turns left) go over a bar stile ahead and proceed with the hedge on your right, through a squeeze stile and out to a green lane in which turn right. Ignore, quite soon, a green lane which comes in from the left. Keep ahead in the wide track for ¼ mile or so to reach a road at the quaintly named hamlet of Blackcat and to rejoin the main walk by crossing the road to a path opposite.

CHIGWELL ROW, HAINAULT FOREST AND LAMBOURNE END

WALK 11

★

3, 5½ or 8 miles (5, 9 or 13 km)

OS Landranger 177

Although considerably smaller than Epping Forest, Hainault Forest, measuring approximately 2 miles long by 1 mile wide, has much to offer. Indeed, many find it preferable to Epping Forest in that there are no roads through it and therefore no traffic noise, and horse riding is mainly confined to the western part. There are fine open glades and picnic areas in secluded spots. For a forest within a dozen miles of London the flora and birdsong are magnificent. To see the gorse in early February, and hear blackbird and thrush, and to sit in south-facing glades sheltered from the wind in February sunshine is to experience the true promise of spring and the pleasures to be had from the forest at all times of the year.

The walk visits Foxborough Farm, where there are rare breeds of domestic animals on display, and the forest lake and goes beyond the forest for the views over London and the beautiful track and field paths to the Norman church of Lambourne, looking out peacefully over a true panorama of Essex.

To reach the starting point take the A12(T) from Wanstead and, after about 5 miles, at traffic lights at Chadwell Heath and with the Moby Dick on the right, turn left on the A112 for Chigwell. Go over two roundabouts and over Hog Hill. On coming down towards the industrial estate on the left you get your first glimpse of Hainault Forest crest away to the right. Go over two sets of traffic lights and just short of further traffic lights on the top of the hill and opposite Chigwell Row church on your right, pull into the car park on the left.

To avoid possible confusion I will first of all describe the full round, giving, as they occur, the turn-off points for the shorter walks. On my map it is the full walk which is arrowed. See note at end for instructions re the medium and short walks.

From the car park just specified cross the road by the traffic lights and go downhill passing the church and some houses on your left. Where the houses end turn left on a track and walk with housing on your left. At the end of the houses turn rightwards on a crossing track with forest on the left. On coming to a further crossing track (with a clearing ahead) turn left (point A) on a gravel track and follow uphill. Later there are iron railings alongside the track. Instead of keeping to the 'obvious' track you can, if you are adventurous, detour into the trees on the left provided you maintain contact with the main 'arterial' track.

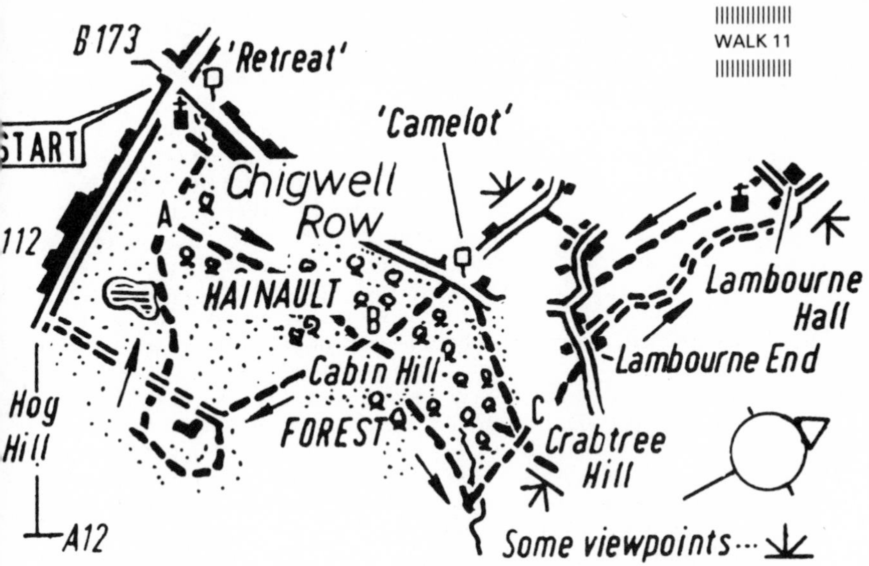

Follow the track for about a mile to a clearing at the top of Cabin Hill. Here are seats on which you can rest and enjoy the view. This is point B, from which five tracks radiate.

For the full walk take the leftmost track (ie turn squarely left from your original approach) past a horse ride on the right at the edge of the forest. In only 50 yards or so turn off rightwards on another of the forest's main paths (Cavill's Walk). In 300 yards or so on this fork off half right, keeping on the track along the ridge with fine views through the right-hand fringe of trees extending southwards over the golf course. In the area to the right of the path there is a series of little bracken-clad dips reminiscent of parts of Surrey and it is well worth leaving the main path (so long as you don't lose contact with it) to explore these.

The track subsequently goes downhill finally running near the right-hand edge of the wood (again with views to the right). The path then bears left and crosses a bridge over a small stream. Here at a wooded angle of the forest turn squarely left keeping just inside the edge of the forest with open countryside to the right. In a ¼ mile and at the top of a rise (Crabtree Hill) you meet a cross track. Here turn right for only 15 yards or so to a stile on the right, where there is a seat commanding a view south-east over grass and towards Havering church and the white water tower seen to the left of this church.

Retrace your way and continue (as if you had turned left without detouring to the stile-with-a-view) and after about 75 yards look out for a narrow path on the right. This runs through bushes and very soon comes out by a stile into the open. This is point C. For the full walk cross the field to a gap in the opposite hedge (to the right of a stile which is buried under a tree) and ahead uphill with hedge on the right. Halfway up the path should veer left to a gap halfway along the hedge ahead but if the field is in crop most people appear to continue beside the hedge and turn left in the corner to the gap. The rearward view ranges over the Thames towards the Kentish hills — a bit industrial but quite impressive.

Turn left on the road reached and just after passing a footpath sign on the left (by a pond) turn rightwards on the signposted bridleway with farm buildings on the right. Veer to the left, to follow a fenced path to the left of a barn and at the end of the fenced path veer right to continue ahead on a green lane. This can be wet in places, but at one particularly waterlogged spot it is possible to detour by using the bank to the right.

The track then bends left with views eastwards over to Epping Forest and half right ahead (over a meadow with a pond in it) towards Ongar and the Roding valley. The path then turns rightwards and passes a wood on the left, after which it becomes narrower and brings you out to a lane elbow.

Here turn left to Lambourne church and then take a field path squarely left, passing a side of the churchyard on your left. Follow, hedge on left, to a gate (note the rear view). Cross the next field to a further wicket gate. Keep ahead (south) passing a pond on your left until, ⅝ mile from Lambourne church, you come out on a road. The mast beside the road is one of a number used to transmit, by radio, messages to London ambulancemen.

Turn rightwards in the road and in 300 yards, and as the road bends squarely right, turn left over a stile. Here is one of the most outstanding viewpoints of this walk. On a clear day such London landmarks as the Post Office Tower (now London Telecom Tower), the Alexandra Palace and the Crystal Palace television aerial can be picked out.

Go downhill, hedge on right, to a lane and turn left uphill walking on the grass verge where possible. The Camelot pub (formerly the Beehive — note the old sign still incorporated into the side of the building) is reached in ⅜ mile.

To continue, cross the car park opposite the pub passing (on the right-hand side of the car park) the pound erected for impounding cattle straying in the forest c. 1904. Take a track southwards through the forest. In ½ mile you reach the 'Clapham Junction' of tracks at the top of Cabin Hill again (point B). *From this point (reached second time round on the long and the medium routes) all the walks follow the same route.*

(**X**) Proceed ahead on the track downhill over grass. This is a favourite spot for tobogganing in the all too infrequent snows we get in this part of Essex. Keep through the left-hand gap on the track over gently undulating country, but all the time descending. In the dip where a track is visible to the left leading ahead turn rightwards through a gap over a horse ride (being careful to watch for horses).

Head leftish over open space to the estate office in the valley. The estate office has leaflets available on the forest including the Woodpecker Walk which we now follow. After visiting the office go up the path between the office and buildings on the left to follow the path on the right through the pens containing the rare breeds of domestic animals which include Highland cattle, longhorn sheep, goats, chickens, Chinese geese etc. There are also peacocks wandering free.

Then return past the office and turn right on a tarmac drive. Beyond the houses at the end of the fence turn right uphill past a waymark (point C on Woodpecker Walk). At point D on Woodpecker Walk veer left to a fence to see the views over the countryside towards Havering. Towards the top of the hill bear to the right with the track, still following waymarks, over a crossing track and at point F on Woodpecker Walk keep inside the fence on your left. The waymarks lead on rightish into the trees downhill keeping to the left side of open trees and on through bushes to finally emerge from the woodland at a very good view and a seat on which to admire it (point G on Woodpecker Walk).

Turn right downhill over an open space to the refreshment building and toilets by a car park. Cross track and keep ahead with the car park on the left to the lake. Turn right with the lake on your left and at the end of the lake continue ahead to go through a gap and turn left with the lake still on your left. On reaching a bridge on the left do not cross but turn right on the track (away from the bridge) for about 5 yards then fork left into the woodland onto a wide track. Go over a transverse horse ride and ahead leftish to and over a gravelled track (used on the outward route).

Follow the track ahead, first through trees then on the left-hand side of a glade with houses on the left. At the end of the housing turn half left on a track into the car park of the Retreat pub. Leave this by the far right-hand corner and follow to the main road. Here turn left back to the crossroads and car park from which you started.

Notes

For the short walk. Proceed to point B and here turn rightwards. Then follow as for full walk, from (**X**) above.

For the medium walk. Proceed to point C. Continue ahead, keeping just inside the edge of the forest, passing houses on your right. Keep on for ½ mile until you come to a road. Here turn left to a road junction with the Camelot on your right. Turn left into the car park opposite and proceed on the grass track (there is a picnic area by the car park) southwards through the forest and in ½ mile you reach the clearing at Cabin Hill (point B) again. Here keep forward and follow the full route, from (**X**) above.

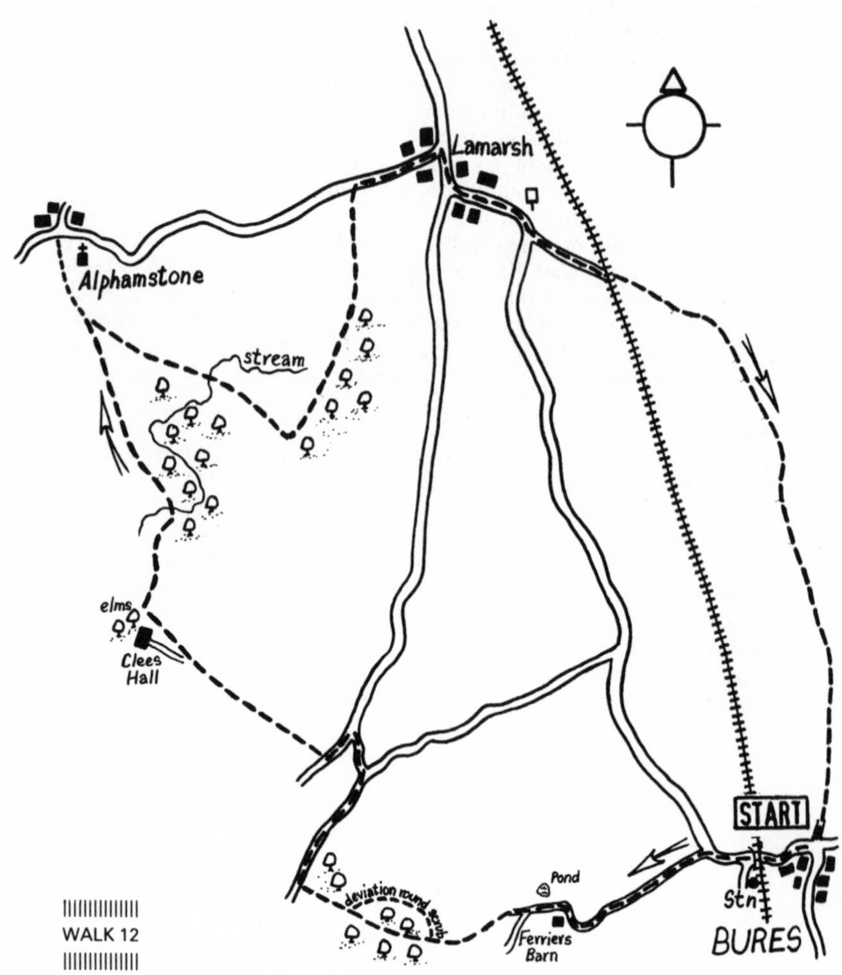

Lamarsh
Alphamstone
stream
elms
Clees Hall
START
Pond
deviation round scrub
Ferriers Barn
Stn
BURES

WALK 12

BURES, LAMARSH AND ALPHAMSTONE

WALK 12

★

6 miles (9.5 km)

OS Landranger 155

Here we have a walk from one of the last villages in Essex right on the Suffolk border. In fact half of Bures is in Suffolk but our walk is purely in Essex. This is mainly a walk on good grassy tracks through and beside woodland and over low rolling hills with secluded valleys and good views.

Bures is situated midway between Sudbury and Colchester on the B1508. To remain in Essex one should park in the high street on the west side of the bridge, but if you venture slightly into Suffolk by crossing the bridge and continue past the church there is a car park by the recreation ground.

From the high street take the road signposted for Lamarsh (with the bridge behind you) walking on the walled path. Pass the station and the Paddocks on the left and proceed ahead under the railway. The road now becomes Lamarsh Hill and beyond Woolpit Downs on the left, where the road bears to the right, continue ahead on a tarmac lane by a bridleway sign. The lane leads on past Ferriers Barn on the left where you then bear left with a pond on the right. Ignore the left fork at a green triangle and continue ahead. About 15 yards before the barn ahead bear left into a field and continue ahead with the barn and hedge on your right. At the end of the hedge continue ahead over a field to the left edge of a belt of trees and go on in the same line parallel to a stream which is about 50 yards to your left.

On coming to a belt of scrub on the left there is a slight problem as the path should go diagonally left through the scrub but it is blocked by a wire fence and the path is overgrown so it seems better at present to continue beside the fence with scrub on your left. In the corner turn right for about 5 or 10 yards to go through a gap at the end of the scrub and fence and turn left steeply downhill with the scrub on your left to turn right onto a wide grassy path in the valley beside a stream.

Follow this path with newly planted trees on its right out to a narrow lane. Turn right uphill and at a T-junction turn left for Lamarsh. Where the lane turns right turn sharp left for Clees Hall. Then by footpath signposts turn right through brick pillars and follow a made-up lane towards the hall. Where the road turns left into the hall by houses on the right the walk continues ahead on a green track on the edge of a field. As you leave the road enjoy, on your left, a reminder of the past glories of Essex — two magnificent fully grown elm trees. (Long may they remain free of the scourge which killed off all our elm trees, namely Dutch Elm Disease.)

There are views of the hall to the left as you reach a corner and bear right on a track towards a wood. At the wood go through a gap ahead and immediately turn right onto a track bearing left round the outside of the wood with newly planted trees beside the track. At the end of the wood turn left on the path through the edge of the wood and out into a field. Continue ahead with trees on your right and at the end of the field go over a track and straight on across a field aiming for a gap at the top of a hill to the left of a belt of trees coming up from the right. Beyond the gap continue ahead on a track between fields to the delightful village of Alphamstone. There are views of the church as you approach up the hill and views to the right over a secluded valley. (Unfortunately there is no public house in Alphamstone but the views may make the detour well worthwhile!)

Retrace your steps from the church and turn left on a track. Where the track bears off to the left downhill the path should go straight across the field to a gap in trees opposite (about 70 yards from the field corner) and should be reinstated but if this is not the case it is possible to follow the track round the field edge to this gap. The path leads ahead into the trees steeply downhill to cross a stream and on steeply uphill to emerge into a field with a wood on the right. Continue ahead uphill on a delightful grassy path not forgetting to look back at Alphamstone church from the top of the hill.

When the wood ends the path should go straight ahead to the field boundary and turn left but it is again possible to follow the track round to this point. Continue gently downhill with a wood on your right, in countryside reminiscent of the foothills of the Sussex Downs, to a road at Lamarsh. A notice on the signpost informs you that this land is included in the Premium Set Aside Scheme.

Turn right past Reynolds on the right and at the T-junction right again, bearing left past a road to Hornes Green and on to or past the Red Lion pub. Just beyond the pub where the road turns right go ahead on a little lane which is signposted as a private road but is also a public footpath. The lane is stony at first then bears rightish beyond a thatched house and old barn on the left. It then passes a strange notice on the right that reads 'Car Park. Proceed quietly!' Beyond a green shed and Kinos Farm on the right the lane becomes grassy. Cross a stile and with care a railway line to cross another stile into a field.

This delightful path now continues downhill, with a hedge on the right, and the river (the boundary of Essex and Suffolk) on your left. At the end of the field cross a stile into a hedged lane bearing right and left round a fallen tree and ahead to a field. Follow a track with at first a hedge on the left and then a belt of fir trees. The path then runs between fields but when a hedge starts on the left leave the track and continue beside it with the hedge on your right. At the end of the field, the path becomes fenced with a wall on the right and leads on round a gate and out to the high road at Bures.

MALDON, BEELEIGH WEIR AND BEELEIGH ABBEY

WALK 13

★

8½ miles (13.8 km) or 3 miles (4.8 km)

OS Landranger 168

Maldon is on the A414 approximately 9 miles from Chelmsford and approximately 10 miles from Kelvedon on the A12. Approaching from Danbury keep on the main road past the Moot Hall and clock tower to go over a mini roundabout and keep ahead to the Rose and Crown on the left. Immediately beyond the pub turn sharp left on a very narrow road (Butts Lane) to the car park, being careful to pick the public car park and not the pub car park. The former is pay and display in the week but free on Sundays.

From the car park return to Butts Lane and turn left, then take a diagonal concrete path to the river Blackwater and turn left with the river on your right to a road at Fullbridge. Turn right over the river and after 25 yards turn left on a signposted footpath between a pub and a wall. Cross a concrete area and go half left up onto the river bank.

Continue under the new bypass with the river on your left and carry on ahead with the golf course on your right. At the end of the golf course (before a bridge ahead) turn left onto the path over the impressive Beeleigh Falls. Beyond the falls you come to a waymark on the Millennium Way where the short walk turns left. (See (**A**) below.)

For the main walk ignore the waymark and turn right on the bridge in front of the lock to turn left on the towpath and follow the canal for about 3 miles to a road at Hoe Mill. Cross the canal by road bridge and shortly (just beyond the mill) turn right on a fenced path on the left of the mill. At the end of the path turn right and immediately left to continue ahead with a hedge on your left. At the corner, cross a stile into an orchard.

Turn right for 25 yards then left by a waymark to go down between rows of trees, aiming for the left side of a house on the far side of the orchard. Cross a stile and follow a fenced path left and right but keeping to the left of, not on, the drive. You later pass a line of conifers on the right and bear right to a stile on the right of the conifers to a road. Turn left and immediately right at the crossroads to turn left immediately before a school, but keep ahead if you require refreshments at the Queen Victoria pub.

Retrace your steps past a school then turn right at the end of the school onto a signposted footpath (No. 19) going downhill with a hedge on your right. In a dip turn left for 12 yards then right on a narrow path

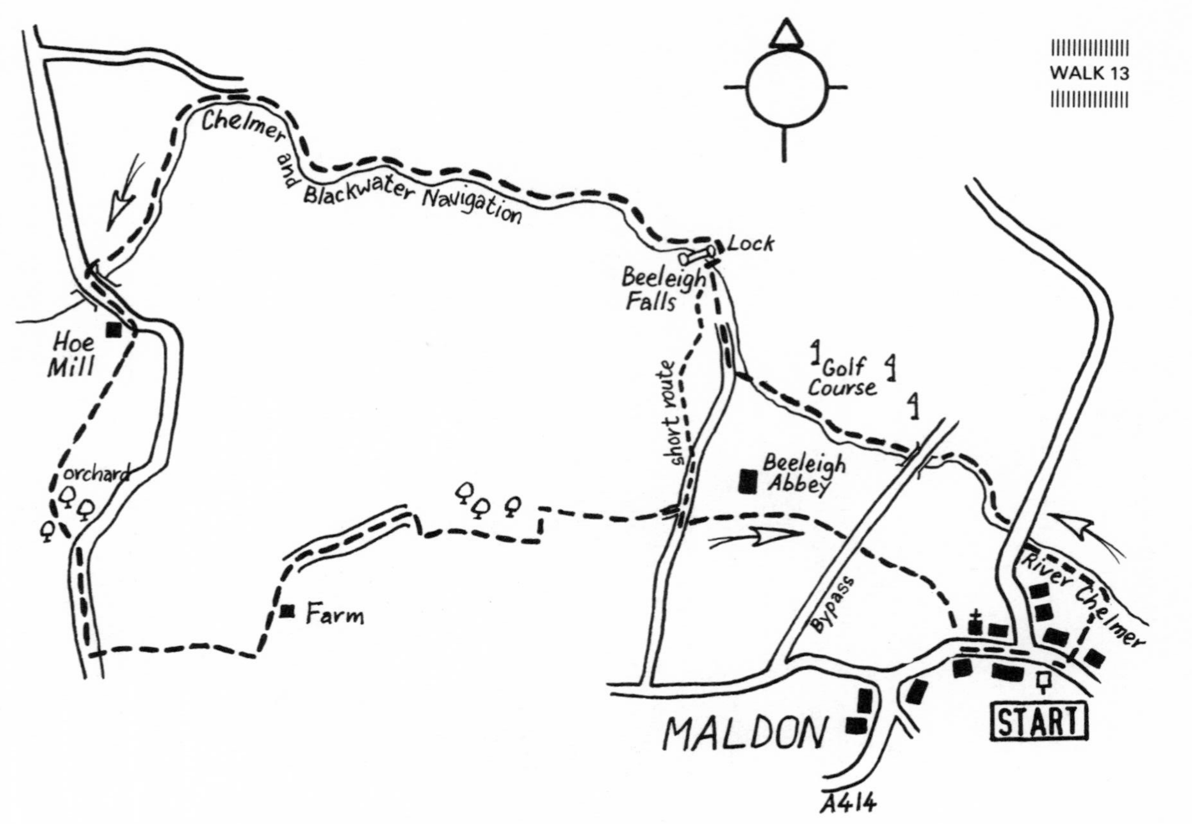

Chelmer and Blackwater Navigation
Lock
Beeleigh Falls
Golf Course
short route
Beeleigh Abbey
Hoe Mill
orchard
Farm
Bypass
River Chelmer
MALDON
START
A414

into a thicket. Cross a bridge and go straight on uphill over a field, on an unploughed strip, to a crossing track and ditch.

Turn left on the track bearing right with it to turn left past (at present) a derelict house to the road junction. Go straight ahead on the road. Follow round a right-hand bend and about 50 yards thereafter if you keep a look out on the right you will see where a spring rises and can be seen flowing even after very dry weather.

Continue ahead to a T-junction where you then turn right for about 40 yards and beyond a house on the left turn left on footpath No. 28 with a garden on the left. Continue over a field to a hedge corner and carry on with the hedge on your left. Cross a house drive and at the end of the garden bear left onto a track which you follow ahead. This runs as a hedged track through woodland and 25 yards beyond the end of the woodland on your right turn right over an earth bridge (between willow trees). Then turn left with a ditch on your left.

Go through a gap in the corner and keep ahead crossing to the left-hand side of a rough grass strip. Keep this strip and later a ditch on your right until you reach a fence and track ahead. Turn left for 40 yards then right over a bridge by Millennium Way waymarks. Go straight ahead over a field to a road where you then turn right. (Continue at (**B**) below.)

(**A**) For the short walk turn left by the waymark on a narrow path through rough woodland. Go through a gate and on over a bridge to a large stretch of open water on your left. Turn right and then left over a big bridge and follow a path to a road. Keep ahead past the site of a mill on your left and past a footpath on the right where the main walk comes in.

(**B**) Take the first turning on your left signposted for Beeleigh Abbey. You pass the entrance to the abbey on your left after which the path becomes a narrow green hedged lane. This leads out to a field where you keep ahead and at the end of the field bear right and left through trees to cross a stile into a narrow fenced path. This leads to the bypass. You can either cross with care or for a pleasanter and safer walk turn left on the path beside the bypass which leads down to the canal, where you turn right under the road bridge then right on the path beside the bypass to rejoin the walk at the top of the steps from the bypass. Follow a fenced path ahead (away from the bypass steps) keeping past an old house on the right which was used as a barracks in the Napoleonic Wars and on along a fenced path which becomes Beeleigh Road with houses to left and right.

At the end of the road cross junctions with care then keep straight on to the high street to turn left past the Moot Hall with clocktower.

At a mini roundabout turn left to a zebra crossing and then right to continue down the high street turning left between Matthews' shop and the Swann Hotel back to the car park.

DANBURY COUNTRY PARK AND LINGWOOD COMMON

WALK 14

★

4 miles (6.5 km)

OS Landranger 167

Note. Although this walk is of very modest mileage, note that non-walking members of the party can be left behind to potter around the country park whilst others do the walk.

Danbury is one of the claimants to being the highest village in Essex. Despite some inevitable latter-day development it certainly enjoys a lovely position since it is surrounded by well-wooded National Trust commons and a country park.

On Danbury Common there are traces of earthworks thrown up not by Ancient Britons but by perspiring Royal Engineers summoned to oppose the expected invasion of these Isles by Napoleon. Marauding Romans, Danes and others had come this obvious way and so, it was thought, would 'Boney'.

It is to be confessed that one needs the eye of an archaeologist fully to appreciate the extent of those earthworks since there is now an overgrowth of bushes. But a notice board on the common draws your attention to them.

Other points of interest are mentioned in the text.

From Chelmsford take the A130 and then the A414 towards Maldon. At the outskirts of Danbury, almost opposite the Bell turn rightwards down Bell Lane on a road signposted to the lakes and to the country park. In ¼ mile, at a T-junction, turn rightwards past a house soon reaching the first of the two car parks, designated as 'Danbury Country Park: Car Park and Picnic Area'.

This is probably the best place to park and, in the description which follows, it is used as the starting point. But there is another, the Lakes Car Park, a little farther on. This is larger and more extensively used, though for these reasons it is likely to fill up first.

Although it is extremely unlikely that, on this walk — even if done as a summer evening one — you will arrive back late, it is as well to check times of car park closing. (On my visit it was 21.45 for the picnic area car park and 22.00 hours for the other.)

From the car park return to the lane in which you turn left and after 25 yards (by a road junction sign) enter a defined path on the right-hand side of the road which bears away rightish on the right-hand side of woodland with extensive views to the right. This leads into an unmade

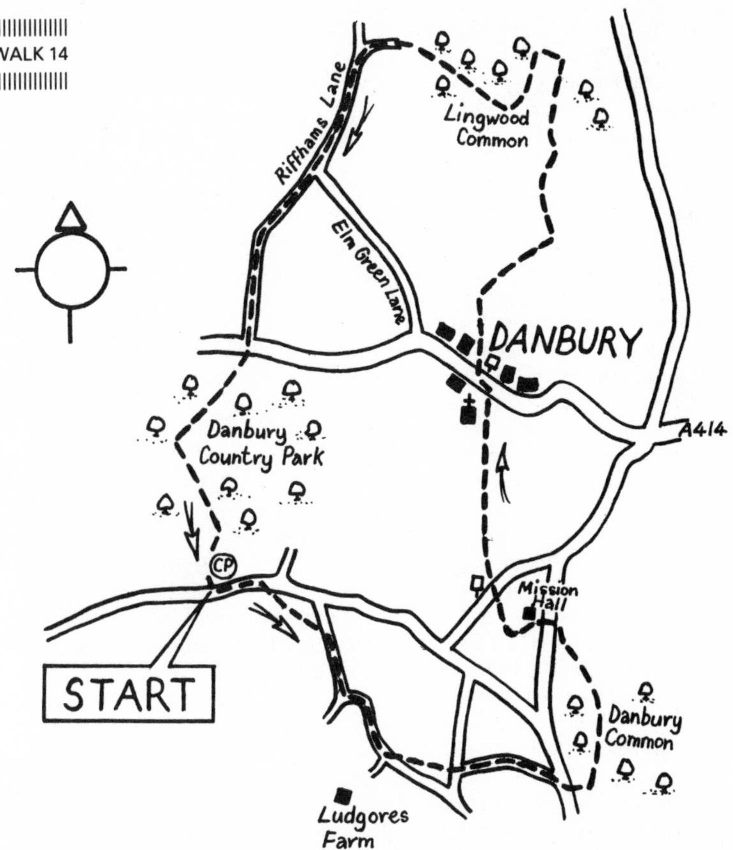

road (Fitzwalter Lane) with a house on the right. Beware stones placed in the path along the edge of the grass outside this house. Continue ahead (ignoring right forks) to a road. Turn left and follow round a right-hand bend.

When the road soon turns sharp left continue ahead into woodland on a path (just to the left of Ludgores Lane sign). After 10 yards turn right downhill on a narrow winding path through the trees to a crossing lane. Cross leftish into Plumptre Lane and continue along this lane. In the far corner where the lane turns left you pass a house called Thatched Cottage. This also dates back to the Napoleonic Wars when it was the home of the officers of the troops who were camped on the common.

Beyond the cottage cross the road onto a track on the common which leads on past a car park on the right and over a crossing track. Continue ahead then turn sharp left with the track past a small pit (or large hole) on the left and after about 10 yards fork left into an open space. Continue ahead over the open space passing a seat on your left and at the end of the space bearing right to and across a road. Continue with a mission hut (now a house) on your right and go ahead for about 50 yards to a manhole cover.

Here turn right on a narrow path between fences into woodland. At a road cross to a path opposite with the Cricketers pub to your left. The path leads steeply uphill towards the church and at the top of the hill pause to look back at the panoramic view stretching from Chelmsford on the right to the Thames estuary to the left.

Although the Danbury church spire is a landmark for miles around and can even be seen, I am told, from the sea (since the church stands on a hill 365 ft high) the prospect of it, from our present position, is somewhat eclipsed by an intervening water tower and aerials.

You may well care to visit the church (if open) since it contains, among other items of much interest, the figures of three Knight-Crusaders carved not in the usual stone but in oak.

To get to the church take the gate on the left. For the ramble route keep straight on to the drive in front of the church and continue in this down to the main (A414) road. Here turn left past the Griffin, of 15th century foundation.

Immediately beyond the Griffin turn right into a public open space owned by Danbury Parish Council. Bear half left past a seat and continue through a gap to turn right onto a narrow footpath leading downhill on the left-hand side of the open space. At the bottom of the hill continue into a meadow where you then turn right with a hedge on your right. At the end of the meadow cross a bridge and continue ahead into woodland to a concrete drive where you turn left.

Where this ends, continue for a few yards to a stile and so on to the wooded Lingwood Common. Go over a transverse path and then half left, uphill, to reach another transverse path. The seat at this point is a good place to rest awhile and enjoy the view.

Turn leftwards on this transverse path (rightwards, of course, if you are getting up from the seat). After 15 yards turn left downhill on a track by a blue arrow on a post which indicates that the path is a bridleway. Be careful to look out for a narrow path on the right in a dip about 5 yards from a crossing stream. Follow this delightful path which is later mainly near the left-hand edge of the woodland out to a road (Riffhams Lane).

Turn left along this lane ignoring, later, Elm Green Lane which comes in from your left and continue to the A414. Cross with care into Danbury Park which is partly a youth camp and partly a country park. Follow the path half right along a line of white topped posts. Towards the end of this path where a stile in a transverse hedge becomes visible there are views to the left of the red brick palace. (The present building, of quasi-Tudor architectural style dates from 1832 and was, for a time, an official residence of the Bishops of Rochester. Presumably these Kentish clerics, like most MPs took care not to reside in their own constituency.)

Here CARE IS NEEDED to double back leftwards at the second white topped post from the stile to pass a tap used by campers. Follow a further line of white topped posts to a gate leading into the picnic area. Keep ahead with the fence on your left to a gap leading into woodland. Cross a bridge and 25 yards thereafter fork left past toilets and back to the car park.

NORTH WEALD AND COLLIERS HATCH

WALK 15

★

5¼ miles (8.4 km)

OS Landranger 167

This is a companion to Walk 18 with which it shares its woodlands and the Roman road.

When I first started writing ramble-route articles over 25 years ago I planned one walk to go all the way from near Epping to Toot Hill (see notes to Walk 18). About midway I found my way barred by impenetrable woodland which made the public bridleway impassable.

As you go along this way today you will find that much of this erstwhile woodland has been completely cleared and is now ploughland. Much of the old woodland still remains, however. Some is still completely wild, some is being reafforested. All is now passable.

To reach the start make for Epping (on the A104 which is continued as the B1393) and just past the town fork off on the B181. Just before reaching the ancient Kings Head turn rightwards for North Weald station.

There is limited parking by the station, otherwise look for it as you approach North Weald.

With your back to North Weald station go forward a few yards and then turn rightwards on a gravelled track which curves back over the railway lines (take care here!). Now follow the clear forward track (with the power line) until in ¼ mile it runs into another farm road (point X).

Still keep ahead to the farm (Cold Hall) in view. Just short of the buildings turn left and then right, outside the buildings and keep straight on with a brick wall and farmhouse on your right. At the corner turn left with a hedge on your right to reach in approximately 200 yards a gate. Here, disregarding the facing ladder stile, turn rightwards on a track towards a wood. On reaching it continue, just a trifle leftwards, over a transverse track, part of a Roman road (note its alignment with a road stretch on another part of this present walk), and continue by the track passing a pond (the preserve of North Weald anglers) on your left.

If this track is muddy after wet weather note that you can soon, albeit permissively, take quite a clear dry path through the trees on the left. Look out for this path if needed. The way is continued ahead as a hedged farm road. In this there seems no escape from any softness in the dip.

So you arrive at farm buildings and a cottage (point Y). If you do not require an inn, turn rightwards at the cottage opposite a water tower on to a hedged path on the right-hand side of a garden. Keep on for ¼ mile to a path joining from the left (point Z) where, as described in due place,

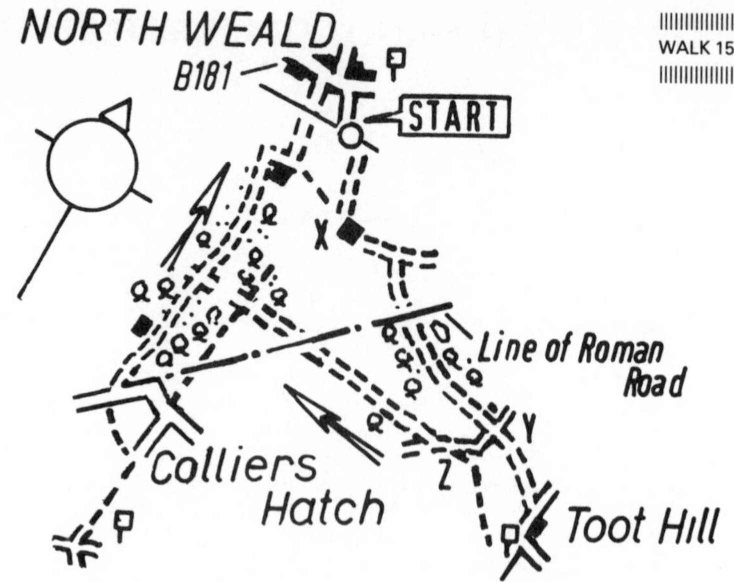

the main ramble is rejoined. Those requiring an inn, however, should ignore the right-hand path just described. Instead, continue ahead, now by a narrow but 'made' lane, to a T-junction.

Here turn rightwards and just after passing a lane on the left you come to the Green Man which has a nice garden. You are at Toot Hill.

Just beyond the pub, turn off, square from the road on a signposted path which starts from a five-bar gate. This path soon bends a little rightwards and proceeds to another stile by a five-bar field gate near the top right-hand corner of the field. Continue with the hedge on your right for 250 yards. Here the hedge ends. From this point bear half left downhill across a small field. On the other side you will find a swing gate beside a small coppice. This is point Z where those taking the short cut rejoin the main route.

Through this gate proceed first with the trees briefly on your left. Then, the now open track goes uphill. In ¼ mile it drops suddenly and steeply, with woodland on the left (the southern part of the wood already traversed earlier in this walk).

Emerging from this, the track continues arrow-like, due west and slightly uphill for another ¼ mile to meet what is currently the dense, 'natural', High Wood. Enter it but in a matter of a few yards—just inside — turn left in a crossing track. Follow out to reach, in ¼ mile, a lane at Colliers Hatch. Here turn left for only a few yards and then turn rightwards for approximately 200 yards. (Here you can make a diversion along this pleasant lane to visit the Moletrap pub for refreshments but this adds about ¼ mile each way to the walk.) Just before the wooden paling fence of a house, Fyrth Tawney, turn right on a signposted footpath across a field aiming slightly right of the right edge of a belt of conifers to the right of a pink house out to a road. Looking to the left and observing how straight this road (another section of the Roman road we met earlier) is, you can obtain an idea of what fine road builders the Romans were.

Cross rightish to a little lane bearing a No Through Road sign. Beyond Mountwood Cottage (which has been seen ahead) the way becomes a magnificent green road, not so rough as the first few yards would suggest. Avoid veering half left. For the first couple of hundred yards or so you will have open country to the right. A wood then comes in on the right. Keep ahead on the green road soon to reach a conspicuous crossing track.

Go over this and continue ahead for a short ½ mile. You then merge with a farm road that comes in from the left. Continue on this, soon to reach farm buildings. Here, just round a sharp right bend you come to a junction. Here you have a choice of ways. The right-hand branch will take you in ¼ mile to a track on your left which will take you back to your parking place.

The little lane going leftwards, however, takes you under the railway bridge and so to the main Epping Road. Here turn rightwards and, whilst noting that the ancient and photogenic Kings Head is in view, turn rightwards again in Station Road.

ONGAR AND STANFORD RIVERS

WALK 16

★

3 or 7 miles (4.8 or 11.2 km)

OS Landranger 167

With measured step and solemn chant the monks of Bury St Edmunds made their way along the forest tracks bearing with them the body of their sainted King Edmund who had been killed in battle against the Danes in AD 807. Now, 1013, the Danes were invading again and, for safety, the body of the martyr was being carried to the walled city of Westminster. The danger past, the body was carried back again.

Among the places the body rested at was a tiny wooden chapel at Greensted near Ongar. Its wooden walls — made from oaks growing when the Romans came — are there today. In the 16th century the church was much refashioned. A chancel, priest's doorway, tower and belfry were added. A century ago a brick footing had to be added to the base of the ancient wooden walls — the oldest in England — as they were much rotted at ground level.

But the Greensted church of St Andrew in its fine sylvan setting remains, basically, a bit of Saxon England and is a place of much pilgrimage.

Ongar — in full, Chipping Ongar (chepe = market) — still remains much of a one-main-street country town.

One way of getting to Ongar is to make for Epping and just beyond the town take the B181 and then the A414. This will bring you to crossroads at the north end of Ongar. Here turn rightwards, past the railway station to Budworth Hall, where there is a good pay and display car park.

From the car park proceed down the path between the car park and Budworth Hall. Cross the bridge over Cripsey Brook, continue ahead to the first hedge leading to the right and turn right beside it. In a field corner go through a gap and head half right over the field corner to a fence and continue ahead with the railway on the right. Go over the bridge, turn right under the railway and over a field to turn left beside Cripsey Brook. Follow this delightful stream to the road where you turn left past the Ruggles Restaurant. On the far side of the restaurant a little lane, initially gravelly, slants off.

Follow this, gently uphill, subsequently round a square left bend and then a square right one, later crossing the railway bridge. You then come to a house (New Barns) on the left and the lane (in which you keep forward) loses its surfacing. A privately-erected notice on a tree informs you that this is a footpath way to Toot Hill and to Greensted church.

A few yards past the house, however, look for and turn leftwards over

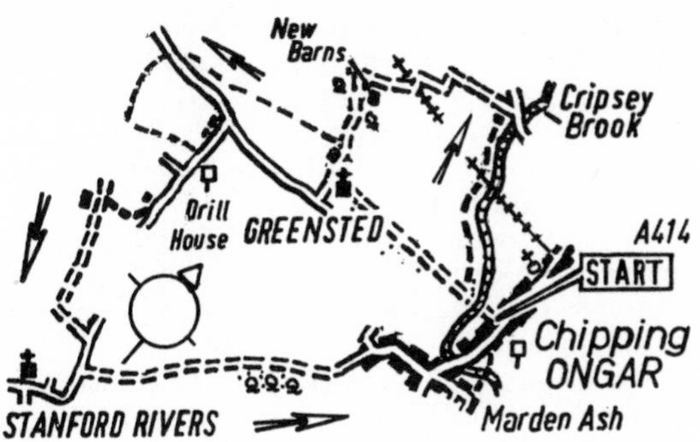

footplanks. After going through a few trees you continue past the back of New Barns. In the field corner turn squarely rightwards. Past a patch of rough trees concealing a little pond you continue, slightly downhill, with an old post and wire fence on your left.

Continue ahead through a gate gap and over an open field to a hedged corner. Here turn left through a field-gate and then rightwards, uphill, to the farm buildings seen ahead, to reach Greensted church.

For the short walk back to Ongar continue past the church and take the footpath on the left beside the drive to Greensted Hall. When the drive goes left continue ahead into a field passing a pond on your right and bearing gradually left to a gate in the transverse hedge. Turn left and in the corner go right beside the hedge and continue ahead to cross the further drive to the hall, looking back from the drive at the view of the hall. Continue ahead on a grassy strip, sadly now all that remains of the once magnificent Long Walk which lost its character when the flanking elms were killed off by Dutch Elm Disease. Follow it through fields and over Cripsey Brook back to the car park.

For the main walk retrace your steps from the church downhill through the farm buildings and towards the bottom of the hill. Look out for a bridge and a footpath sign on the left. Follow this path beside the hedge on the right which in late May is awash with the sight and scent of the white hawthorn blossom. The path leads through the edge of fields and on beside a wood to a road.

Cross leftish to a footpath with a sign for the Essex Way (a long distance footpath from Epping to Harwich). After 200 yards cross a stile on the left and follow the path beside a hedge on the right and a bank on the left. The path bears to the right uphill (with a stable block on the left) over stiles and after crossing the last stile (where the hedge on the right ends) turn left beside the hedge. You pass a pond on the left (behind a hedge) and thereafter keep a look out for a narrow path (where the hedge starts to bear right) leading ahead through a narrow gap in the hedge to a road opposite the Drill House pub.

I expected to see, depicted on the signboard, a mid-Victorian type of Volunteer in his elegant uniform; one who had come out to practise musketry on a nearby rifle range. But no, the 'drill' shown on the signboard is of a different type — and it isn't an electric drill. I'll leave you to discover what it is.

Turn right past the inn, disregarding a right-hand turn. About ¼ mile past this latter, and immediately past a farm (Newhouse) on the right, cross a stile on the right (opposite a gap on the left leading into a new plantation) and follow the fence on the left. Cross a second stile and then head rightish over a field to a stile on the left of a tall tree. Turn right with a hedge on the right and in the corner ignore a bridge ahead and turn left. At a gap on the right change to the other side of the hedge and continue with the hedge now on your left. The path, passing a bungalow, becomes enclosed for a few yards and brings you out to a transverse track at Coleman's Farm.

Take care here not to go through the immediate left-hand gap. Instead, go forward two or three yards and then turn left on a slightly sunken track headed by a bar inscribed 'Bridleway'.

Do not be put off by initial muddy spots. The way becomes drier and is clear. In fact I was glad to find on my visit that it had just been cleared. This 'green' way is much better than taking the metalled lane into Stanford Rivers.

You subsequently cross, by a good little bridge, a stream (a tributary of the Roding) and after 75 yards look out for a gap on the right where a hedge runs off to the right. Go through the gap on the left-hand side of this hedge and head diagonally uphill on a defined path to a projecting hedge corner. Turn left with the hedge and houses on your right and continue ahead to a lane at Stanford Rivers church.

At the crossroads which soon follow turn left. Follow round a left bend (here disregarding a prominent rightward track). A little farther on, however, immediately before cottages (at present being rebuilt), turn in rightwards on a wide track (or farm road). The track gently rises. Before you get to the power line be sure to look back at the church now in the distance.

After ½ mile the farm road turns rightwards. At this point *keep straight on*. The way is, at first, just as wide as before but grassy. You then pick up a wood on your right. Halfway along this the way suddenly becomes footpath-like albeit quite clear. In the field corner continue through a neck of woodland and on again (the way again becomes a track) with a hedge on your right.

It soon becomes a little hedged lane with latter-day housing of Ongar in view. Continue past the school out to a road elbow. Here keep forward (slightly right) passing Fairfield Road on your left. At the T-junction by the Two Brewers you have a choice of ways.

(a) Simply turn left, over the Cripsey Brook and uphill along Ongar's high street, back to the car park.

(b) At the Two Brewers junction turn *rightwards* and very soon take the first left-hand turn.

Where, in ¼ mile or so, this way bends rightwards, take a footpath on the left.

This goes up to a concrete footbridge over the Cripsey Brook and continues quite clearly towards the church in sight. You go directly over a crossing road and then go through the churchyard and a very photogenic corner of old Ongar, out to the high street. Here turn rightwards to the car park.

MILL GREEN AND BLACKMORE

WALK 17

★

4 or 8 miles (6.5 or 13 km)

OS Landranger 167

As a retort, 'Go to Jericho!' is now rather dated, though its implication is still understood. We are asked to believe, however, that Henry VIII sometimes came to Jericho Priory at Blackmore to escape the cares of court and in answer to all enquiries as to where the King was, courtiers often replied, ambiguously 'He has gone to Jericho' knowing that the lascivious prince was more likely to be at a bordello. Or, conversely, when the King was particularly cantankerous, courtiers might murmur, *sotto voce*, 'I wish he would go to Jericho!'

On the optional extension of this round you can take the hint literally and go to Jericho, an old red-brick mansion built on the site of Jericho Priory, close by the interesting church of Blackmore.

Contrary to the normal custom, I am treating the shorter walk as the main one. It goes almost entirely over beautiful woodland tracks which, except, obviously, after much rain, should not be difficult underfoot. The optional route is also very worthwhile as Blackmore is a beautiful village with a chance of refreshment at the Bull pub. The route gives a chance to walk on part of the St Peter's Way (a long distance footpath between Ongar and Bradwell on Sea). It also includes wild and lovely woodland tracks.

To arrive at the start, get on to the B1002 at the Brook Street interchange and continue through Brentwood to Ingatestone. Here turn off for Fryerning and continue into Mill Green. Alternatively, use the Brentwood bypass and turn off at Ingatestone. Continue past the Cricketers pub on the right and just beyond it park on the edge of the green on the left.

Assuming you have come from the Fryerning direction as just described and have parked on the edge of the green continue ahead down the road with the car park on your left. Disregard (left) a bridleway signpost opposite a builder's hut. Just past Woodside Cottages (1836) and Woodside House which follows, turn left to a footpath signpost lying just off the road. This is actually a public bridleway as a sign you will subsequently see at its far end indicates.

The wood you now enter is currently a delightfully mixed one of old oak, chestnut, holly, birch, etc. In these days of increasing conifer commercialization, enjoy it while you may!

Almost at once the path divides. Take the leftmost branch. After being a bit vague for a few yards, it widens out appreciably and drops gently to a small stream where, of course, you can expect to find

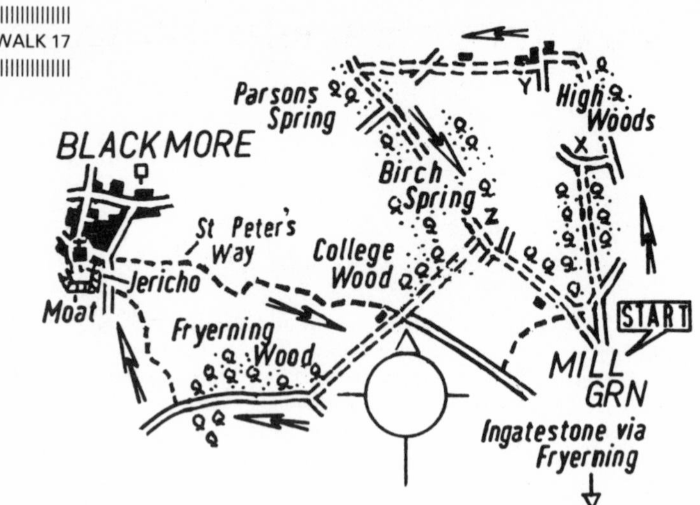

hoof-pounded mud after rain. I skirted this softness without trouble by circling a little to the right.

The track now gently rises and brings you, by a slight right bend, to a gap (much pounded) and so to an open track. Follow this over the field to a lane (point X).

For the basic route *turn rightwards* (but see *Note* which follows). Quite soon where the road bends rightwards take a signposted bridleway on the left. In theory this should slant half left across the cropped field. In practice it goes squarely across to the wood seen ahead. Here you meet quite a deep wide drainage ditch. Turn leftwards along this (wood to your right). Follow out through a hedge gap en route to a farm. Keep on, disregarding a rightward track, out to a transverse lane. Here turn left and quite soon turn rightwards in Matsons Lane (so marked) and point Y.

Note: The track just mentioned is well used by horseriders who quickly remake it should it have been thinned by ploughing. I came this way just after ploughing and had no difficulty at all with it but it may be noted that an alternative way is to turn left at point X. You soon go round a sharp right bend and Matsons Lane is subsequently found on the left.

Either way go down the pebbly Matsons Lane. Past the timber yard, the way, alongside a wood, becomes 'green'. Before it has time to become too soft, however, it becomes semi-'made' and past the photogenic Barrow Farm, with its willow-fringed pond, it becomes a firm drive soon bringing you to a transverse lane.

Cross directly over. The track opposite has, technically, only footpath status. It is followed out, very clearly, just inside the right-hand edge of the wood to a concreted drive. Here turn left to a road junction. Cross the road and take the signposted track through the wood (Birch Spring: Spring being a name — possibly more common in Hertfordshire than Essex — for a wood).

Keep straight ahead to where the wood ends (point Z). Those taking the Jericho detour see notes which follow. For the basic walk keep ahead on a hedged track. Take care not to veer rightwards here. You pass a timber yard (the second one today). Disregard a left-hand track. Keep on by the little lane (pot-holed but seemingly rock hard compared with previous tracks!). Where, at more cottages, this bends sharply left, go round the bend for only a few yards and then resume your forward way (with the electricity line) over the open green, back to your starting point.

Extension to Jericho (Blackmore)

From point Z, turn right on a hedged track to a crossing track. Cross over this and continue on your present hedged track to a road where you then turn right. About 200 yards beyond a house on the right (at the end of the wood on the right) turn right over a bridge and stile. Head diagonally left to a projecting hedge corner and beyond it go half right to the far right-hand corner of the field. Turn right over a ditch (no footbridge) and continue with a hedge on your left for about 200 yards to a large oak tree with a line of three oaks running out beside it into a field on the left. Cross a ditch (no footbridge) and continue with these three oak trees on your left. Beyond them head diagonally over a field aiming for the petrol station visible over the hedge (to the right of a delightful house and Blackmore church) and so out to a road. Turn right and shortly left into the village.

You pass a delightful village sign by the duckpond and the stocks on the green. At the centre of the village at the crossroads turn left soon passing the Bull pub and also Jericho Priory on your left just before reaching the church (note spire). Retrace your steps to the crossroads and turn right repassing the duckpond and village seat.

At the T-junction turn left for 40 yards. Here (on St Peter's Way) turn right on a signposted footpath across a field aiming for the right-hand edge of tall trees (to the right of a solitary oak) and a gap on the right-hand side of a pond. Cross an earth bridge and turn left for 20 yards to a field corner, then turn right with a hedge on the left. At the next hedge corner turn left to a further corner then right. Follow the hedge on the left to a gap on the left where you turn left on a track across a field, passing a pond on the left to join a track near a hedge corner. Turn right with the hedge on the left, follow the track over a stile beside a gate and on through a wood (ignoring a path leading off to the right to a house). Beyond the house the track bears right over the transverse lane on which you started the walk. It then continues as a tarmac lane. Pass Fryerning House on your right and then a road also on the right signposted to Ongar.

Continue down the road ahead passing (at present) a telephone box. Turn left up a track by a footpath sign past a white weatherboard house. Keep ahead over three stiles with a hedge on the right and passing a small pond on the left, keep ahead to a stile in a dip. This leads into a hedged track with a pond on the right and then over a stile at the end of the track into a field. Head uphill to a stile in the corner just to the right of two houses. Keep ahead (right) along a track, and in 50 yards fork right, by a footpath sign, over the green and back to the car park.

EPPING AND BEACHET WOOD

WALK 18

★

6½ miles (10.4 km)

OS Landranger 167

To the east of Epping lies a still very extensive woodland area. In my younger days it was possible to walk in a straight line for nearly 3 miles through woodlands from Gernon Bushes over to Toot Hill. The eastern part of this extensive woodland (Ongar Park Wood, see Walk 15) has now been cleared but, as we shall see on this walk, much of the western part remains; some still in its natural state but gradually being reafforested.

We also pass through parkland and farmland. At the end we go through part of Epping Lower Forest thus adding to our knowledge and appreciation of London's wonderful woodland.

To arrive at the start take the A104 to the Wake Arms junction and continue by the B1393 into Epping. There is a free car park at the north end of the town in Stonards Hill recreation ground. To reach this take the road opposite the green signposted Abridge and after approximately 20 yards (opposite a layby) turn left into the car park.

Epping is also on the London Underground Central Line from London. From the station turn left uphill to the high street where you turn right through the town past the new town hall. Opposite the green turn right on Stonards Hill to the car park.

From the car park go over the grass diagonally (avoiding anybody playing football) to the right-hand corner of a small running track to turn left between the running track and a hedge. A fenced path leads past the football pitch and hospital and on across a field to a bridge over the railway. Here admire the views to your right before following a fenced path to a road. Keep ahead (right) and in the corner continue along a path between houses to a road. Cross to a track with a notice on the right indicating the church car park.

Beyond a hall on the right, cross rails and turn right by an Essex Way waymark. The path bears round to the right downhill then left along the right edge of a wood. Pass a manhole on the left and after a further approximately 75 yards (immediately after a dip) look out for a gap in holly bushes on the right to turn right past a waymark into a field. Enjoy the very fine view, well worth lingering over if the visibility is good. The church in the middle distance is that of Theydon Garnon.

Continue downhill with a hedge on your right, subsequently through a hedge gap and on again with a hedge still on your right. In this second field the official right of way cuts a corner but the vast majority of users nowadays, especially if the field is in crop, seem to follow the hedge on

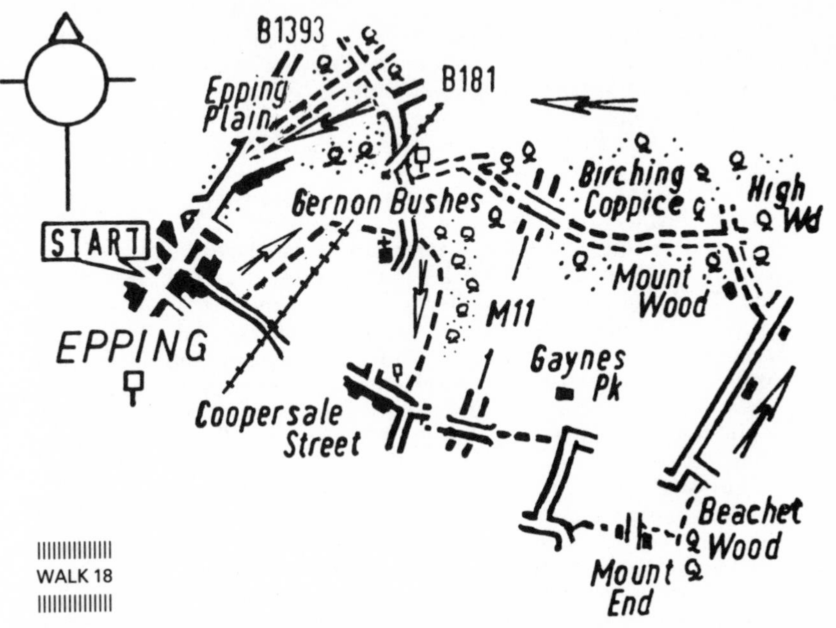

WALK 18

their right to the corner and then turn left for about 50 yards to a stile (which can be seen ahead as you come down the last-mentioned field), and then turn right with, again, a hedge on the right.

At a corner then met turn left and right through a gate and across a meadow to a stile giving exit to a road. Do not, however, enter the road (unless you need the Theydon Oak pub which lies just to the right) but turn left on a drive and then enter, by a swing gate on its right, a signposted foot and bridlepath.

You soon go through another swing gate and over a rivulet. Then, rising gently and with a fence on your left, you come to and cross the lofty footbridge which spans the M11.

Continue with a wire fence on your left passing, over to your left, Gaynes Park mansion. You come out on a lane elbow. Here turn sharply rightwards, downhill. On reaching a transverse lane turn left but in 50 yards or so, where the lane turns squarely rightwards, turn left on a track which, after a half-right bend, becomes unhedged. Follow the defined path to a bridge in the narrow gap in the crossing hedge and continue ahead with a ditch on your right to pass to the left of the barn and exit to a lane in a gap between houses.

Turn left and in only a few yards turn rightwards over a stile (with a concrete footpath sign). I found on my visit that the path was quite clear, running at first with a house on the right, up to a wood. Here turn left with Beachet Wood on your immediate right. The undulating path (with a ditch to cross en route) gives good views towards Epping Town.

You come out on a road in which you turn left for a short distance to a

T-junction. Here turn rightwards. You are now on the line of the Roman road to Dunmow and have good views all round.

In just over ¼ mile you pass a farmhouse on your right and a little after this you pass a modern house also on the right. Just past this you come, on the left, to a tiny lane marked No Through Road. Turn in here.

As far as the red and white 'Mountwood' the byway is surfaced but beyond this you are on a typical Essex green lane.

You then enter a wood (as distinct from isolated trees) and, about ¼ mile from 'Mountwood' come to a definite transverse track. Here turn left. There will at first be conifer plantations either side.

Keep absolutely straight ahead. In about ¾ mile from the T-junction last mentioned, you recross the M11 by a bridge and keep ahead until you reach, fairly soon, a transverse drive. Here turn left, and keep ahead up the main fairly gravelly path (ignoring paths to the left and right) to join a road leading ahead to a T-junction at the Gernon Bushes pub.

Turn right under the railway to the main road. Cross with care to a track opposite leading into Epping Forest (the Old Stump Road which at one time was the main road from Harlow to Epping) and follow to a well-defined crossing track. Turn left on this and follow it out through gradually thinning forest to where it reaches the angle of the Epping and Harlow roads (by traffic signals). Here continue ahead over the junction and along the road to Epping. The first road on the left leads back to the car park while the road ahead continues into the town for shops, refreshments and the station.

KELVEDON HATCH AND STONDON MASSEY

WALK 19

★

5½ miles (9 km)

OS Landranger 167

This is a pleasant, varied, short walk along lanes, drives, field ways and woodland tracks. Stondon Massey is associated with William Byrd (died 1623), a much respected name in the history of British music. He wrote:

Since music is so good a thing
I wish all men would learn to sing.

So it's 'Sing as we go' on this walk.

To reach the start take the A12(T) almost to Brentwood and at a large interchange leave it to continue ahead into the town. At crossroads here turn left on the A128, soon crossing the A12(T) by a flyover. About 3 miles farther you come into Kelvedon Hatch. The 'hatch' part of the name signifies, of old, a forest entry.

Soon after passing the Eagle on your left turn rightwards in School Road. Discreet parking is possible just beyond the school.

About 200 yards up School Road from the main road you will find Mill Lane on the right. Go down this. It is currently unmade and residential at first. By a water tower it bends rightwards to the main road along which you originally came. Turn left for about 100 yards. Opposite the Eagle turn left along Eagle Lane, ignoring the adjacent Swan Lane.

Eagle Lane is residential for a short distance but soon becomes an earth track (too bumpy for cars). This tree-lined way is followed out to a lane elbow (School Road, in fact). Here turn rightwards passing the prominent radio relay station.

At a tiny triangle disregard a left-hand road. Where, soon after, the main road swings right, *continue ahead* by the now drive-like traffic-restricted little road.

Where this runs out to a road elbow, continue forward past The Soap House on your left disregarding a track running left beside its hedge. Then a few yards beyond it enter a field through a gap by a footpath signpost. Facing away from the road head half right to a projecting hedge corner where away to your left you will observe a clump of trees surrounding a pond. Follow the hedge on your right passing a group of electricity poles on your way to the field corner. Turn right onto a narrow path and left by a fence being careful of the drop on your left and broken parts of the fence on your right. This leads out to a road opposite the Bricklayers Arms at Stondon Massey.

You *could* — see the map — now reach Stondon Massey church (like

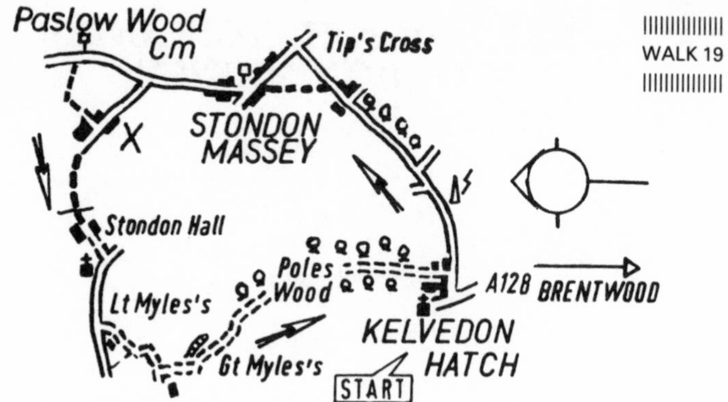

many in Essex a fair way from its village) by turning left and later disregarding a leftward branch. But to enjoy (at the expense of a few very slight hazards of the kind that are almost normal on the average country walk) a footpath stretch, proceed as follows.

Take the Nine Ashes Road passing the Bricklayers Arms on your left and a recreation ground with welcome seats on your right. In ¼ mile you come upon Woolmongers Lane on the left. Here you have an option. The road ahead leads to the Black Horse at Paslow Wood Common with fine views and a charming footpath walk to point X but if you turn left in Woolmongers Lane you reach point X directly.

Assuming you prefer footpath walking and have gone ahead to the Black Horse turn left opposite it on a signposted footpath. The way appears to be down a hedged lane but as this becomes a little overgrown it may be necessary, towards the end of the hedged lane, to walk on the drive beside it.

Where the drive enters the bungalow ahead go ahead on a path on the right-hand side of the bungalow with a garden fence on the left. Pass the gate on your right in the corner and go ahead for a few yards leftish to a stile into a field.

Head ¼ left to a stile (concealed in a hedge corner) aiming for a black shed seen ahead behind a hedge. Turn left over a stile and carry on with a hedge on the left and later buildings on the right to a road where you turn right to point X which is situated where the lane turns sharp right.

There is a footpath sign pointing down a drive but it is misleading as in only a very few yards you turn left over a stile. Head diagonally downhill, aiming for the church on the hill opposite, across fields and over stiles to enter a track in the far corner of the last field. Follow the track to the buildings of Stondon Hall Farm continuing between them to a crossing track where you turn left and right on a lane passing houses and the church on your right and out to a road.

Turn right and repassing the church you come in ¼ mile to the black outbuildings and the white farmhouse of Little Myles. Continue for a further couple of hundred yards or so and turn left on a track. After 150 yards on the far side of a field go through a gap and turn right on a transverse hedged track. Ignore paths to left or right and keep ahead on the main track which later bears leftwards towards Great Myles whose turreted farm block can be seen ahead. Go leftward just before the buildings, passing by various bits of farm machinery.

Be careful where the track turns rightwards into Great Myles and keep ahead with a hedge on your right down to a little bridge with mellow brick parapets.

Over the bridge turn left on a grassy track with wire, succeeded by a ditch, on your left. Subsequently cross this ditch to reach a stile in the corner of the field. Continue forward with a woodland fringe on your immediate left. I found the way clear and comparatively lightly hoof-marked for this is a public bridleway. If you come immediately after ploughing you may think that the way has been shaved a little too closely. But at least part of the width lies along the rough grass strip on the left.

By a hedge gap you enter the next field and soon, by another hedge gap, enter a further field. So you continue, with a small stream on your left. In theory the right of way goes along the other side of the stream but a slight re-alignment (quite clear) seems to have been made. Some 50 yards or so before a hedge joins on the right (at a point where the wood swings slightly right uphill) the path bears left into the wood and right beside a stream.

Now be a little careful! Avoid any temptation to take any path, however clear and well marked, except the one specified — one which incidentally, runs practically due south.

Keep by (or very near) the stream (or its channel should it be dried up in high summer). Before long you will come to quite a high mound. I can only presume that, at one time, there were gravel pits here. Children with the party will surely be tempted to clamber to the top but adults will note carefully that though this mound has to be circled in an anti-clockwise direction, *the original forward direction (by the stream) must be resumed.* Read that again!

You will now be on a kind of green lane. A little beyond this I can only presume that the original old track has become completely overgrown since it is necessary to shift a *little* to the right (avoid going too much so) and then resuming the forward way. If ever you are in doubt note that the radio relay station seen from time to time ahead gives infallible direction.

A little later follow a clear path left and right over the stream tributary thus resuming your former direction being careful not to mistake the tributary for the main stream and thus following it rightwards. Thus you follow a good and pretty path along a neck of woodland and then just inside the right-hand edge of the woodland. So you arrive back at School Road and to your starting point. Towards the end of this walk you may find some motorcycle scrambling going on, but this is only likely at weekends.

RAMSDEN HEATH AND KILN COMMON

WALK 20

★

4½ miles (7 km)

OS Landranger 167

Hedged green lanes and a glimpse of the extensive Hanningfield Reservoir (or Water) are points of particular interest on this walk.

From London take the A12(T) to Gallows Corner near Romford and continue along the A127(T) towards Basildon. On reaching the junction with the A176 turn north along this latter road to Billericay. Drive through the town joining the B1007. A couple of hundred yards beyond the parish church the road diverges. Here branch off the B1007 towards Ramsden Heath crossing the railway line by a bridge and soon after to have a hospital on your left. (If by any chance you find the railway station on your left you have come too far along the B1007.)

About a mile from the town centre the road bends right. Branches to the left and to the right are passed. Another mile brings you into Ramsden Heath.

Two hundred yards beyond the Nag's Head and by a metal church turn leftwards into Mill Lane. Park discreetly in Mill Lane.

Having parked the car proceed, now on foot, down Mill Lane. Soon the village is left behind and the lane becomes a hedged track. In ½ mile disregard a branch to the left. Keep straight on, past Common Farm for another ¼ mile to arrive at an elbow of country lane with a green lane (which you disregard) on the left.

Keep forward (continuing the Mill Lane direction). You soon get glimpses of the extensive Hanningfield Water (or Reservoir) over to the right and on your left you have a wood, the site of an ancient British Camp.

On approaching a brick and weatherboarded farm go rightwards of it (off the lane) on to a concrete track for a few yards only and then rightwards again (before reaching newish battery buildings) on to a green track.

This soon bears rightwards and just past the farm buildings you branch off left along the foot of a bank with the battery buildings on top and with a wood on your right, ignoring a waymark pointing ahead.

Continue into woodland soon crossing a footplank over a ditch and through what, on my late summer visit, I found to be a fine blackberry-gathering ground. (Please do not trespass into the wood.) Cross a second footbridge and go ahead for a few yards to a gravelled track along which go leftwards and coming out to a gateway with the name Roseberry Cottage (on its far side) continue to a metalled lane.

Here turn left for a couple of hundred yards and then turn off

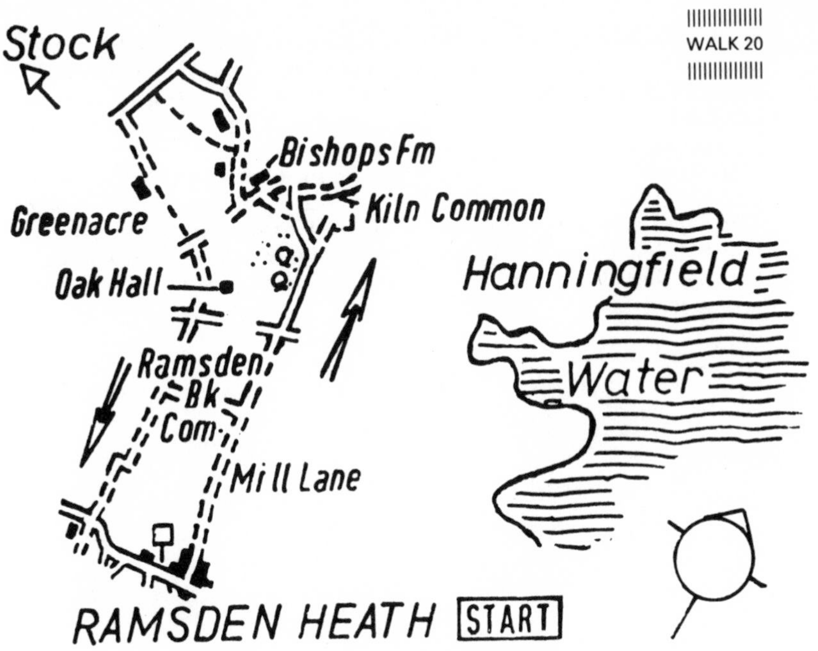

rightwards on an unmade lane soon coming out on to a metalled lane with Bishops Farm (so marked) opposite.

Here turn left for about 30 yards then right on the stoney Brittons Lane (so marked) and continuing ahead to a point about 30 yards beyond a name board (Stock Farm). Here turn left over a stile into a fenced path which almost immediately turns left with a paddock on the left and a ditch on the right. Continue past the barn on the left being careful of a drainage ditch cut inthe path. Cross a bridge and stile and turn right with a hedge on the right. At the end of the field cross a stile and follow a track with a barn on your left out to Marigold Lane where you then turn left.

At a further junction turn left ignoring the footpath signpost opposite along the quaintly-named Small Gains Lane (a name to join Starveacre, Cold Comfort, Rats Castle, Dolittle, Doghouse and other gems of bucolic wit).

In 300 yards or so, turn left down Greenacre Lane (conveniently named as such). On coming to a farm, do not enter the yard. Instead continue ahead (left of the farm). At first the way is lush and grassy but a clear path develops along the edge of a wood and brings you out to the transverse Goatsmoor Lane (marked as such). Cross this leftish to enter the stoney track signposted as a public bridleway and bearing a signboard proclaiming that Oak Hall lies along this way.

In 200 yards, by the gate of the said Oak Hall, the track bends half rightwards and becomes earthen. A hundred yards farther on a transverse track is crossed and you keep straight along the hedged bridlepath. Here you have a choice of either continuing ahead for a little over ½ mile and following the track round a right-hand bend then after about 50 yards turning left on the track out to a road. This gives you the chance to turn left past the Nag's Head pub for refreshment and continuing on to Mill Lane and your car.

In view of the amount of traffic on the road however it is pleasanter and safer to continue ahead on the track to a second transverse crossing where you turn left. At the end of the track turn right on a transverse crossing (Mill Lane) and retrace a little of your outward route to the car. (For the Nag's Head continue ahead to the crossing road where the pub is only just round to the right.)

CLAVERING, STICKLING GREEN AND ARKESDEN

WALK 21

★

6 miles (9.3 km)

OS Landranger 167

This walk is set amongst the gently rolling hills near the Hertfordshire border. The simplest way to approach Clavering is from Newport which is on the B1383 between Bishops Stortford and Great Chesterford. Go west for 3 miles on the B1038 passing the Cricketers on your right, and the village green and Fox and Hounds on your left on your way to the post office on your right where there is some parking space.

Walk back along the B1038 for a short distance then turn left and go along a road with a traffic sign 'Ford'. There are some delightful old houses here, one a small timber building with a thatched roof. Turn right and go straight ahead towards an even smaller house.

Where the road bears left to the ford cross the footbridge to the right, then by the footpath sign opposite, go through a gap in the houses, over two stiles and on to a grassy track between fields. Away to the left are two red brick cones, formerly windmills. It is a gentle climb up to the ridge where a transverse path is crossed before an equally gentle descent to the rear of houses at Stickling Green. DO NOT cross the footbridge but turn left and follow the path above the stream as it curves around the back of the houses to the road.

Turn right at the road, cross the red brick bridge and turn left to go along a broad farm track alongside a stream. The walk along this shallow valley is particularly delightful when the fields on the right are full of golden wheat rising to the green woods above. After about ¾ mile the broad track turns right but a sleeper bridge enables you to cross the ditch and continue along a grassy headland. At the next ditch there is a waymark post but no bridge. However it is an easy scramble across, then shortly after the path reaches Clavering Farm which you pass on your left.

Turn right at the waymark post just after the farm and ascend the field to a corner where two hedges meet. Continue along the field edge to a T-junction where there is a waymark post. Turn right and continue along the field edge to where (although the map shows the path as passing to the left of the farm) a waymark post directs you through Chardwell Farm.

Continue until there is a hedge on your left, then after 100 yards go through a wide gap and across a field to some trees, Westmead Grove.

WALK 21

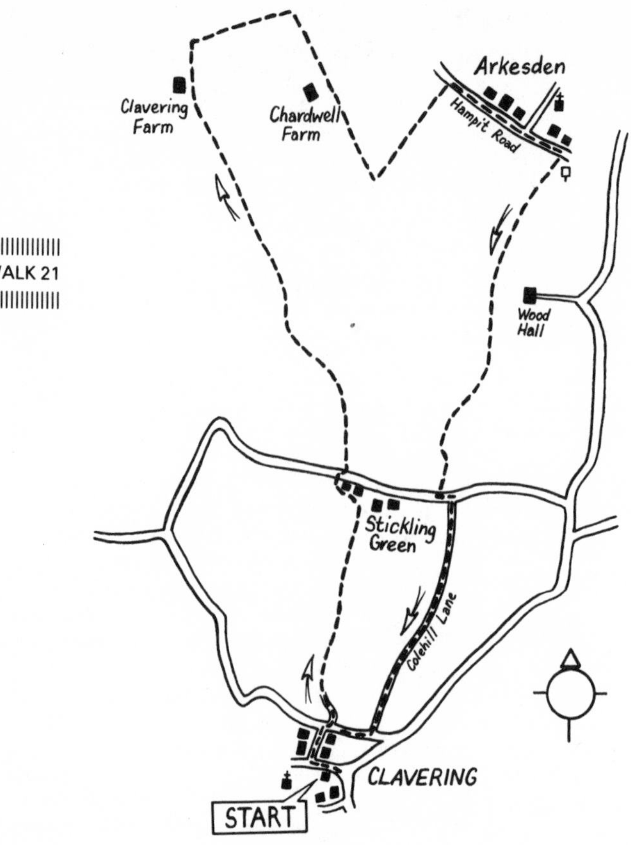

Turn left and descend a field edge path to Hampit Road. Turn right for Arkesden (a really delightful village) where the Axe and Compasses will be found on the right.

From the Axe and Compasses retrace your steps for a short distance to turn left on a signposted footpath by the Arkesden Parish Council notice board. Ascend the footpath along the field edge, then go through a short wooded section where a wide track is crossed, and after crossing a track from Wood Hall the path starts to descend gently. Crossing a transverse footpath at the end of the trees one of the Clavering windmills now appears ahead on the right. Continue with the hedge on your left and where a broad track swings right go straight along a grassy headland. Turn left in the corner and go through a gap in the hedge then over a crude corrugated iron bridge. Turn right, go over a stile and across a field then follow a fence left and right to a road.

Turn left and walk 100 yards to a byway on the right. The byway, Colehill Lane, crosses a red brick bridge then goes up to a transverse track. Clavering village with its square church tower is now ahead. Descend gradually to the village where you turn right back past the ford to the post office.

WITHAM, SILVER END AND FAULKBOURNE HALL

WALK 22

★

6 or 8 miles (9.6 or 12.8 km)

OS Landranger 168, 167

Witham, which is situated midway between Chelmsford and Colchester, has grown over the years since I first knew it but has in its surrounding countryside a fine network of tracks and green lanes. Here is an opportunity to explore these, visit Silver End and also view the magnificent Faulkbourne Hall. The return through the new tree plantation and small pastures gives us a reminder of the Essex countryside before the days of prairie farming. A contrast between the old and the new as we pass through the northern outskirts of the town.

From London turn off the A12 beyond Hatfield Peveril signposted for Witham. At the second set of traffic lights (in the shopping parade) turn left for the station. Cross the railway and almost immediately (beyond pedestrian traffic lights) fork left past a church on the right. Cross a bridge over the river Brain and park in the Spring Lodge Community Centre car park keeping as far as possible on the part of the car park bordering the road.

Return to the road and turn left soon reaching Chipping Hill (the word Chipping being the old word for a market). On reaching a T-junction (the B1018) turn right to cross the main road by the traffic lights and turn left to the station. Almost immediately fork right to pass in front of the station and continue downhill. Follow the road round a sharp left-hand bend and in about 50 yards turn right on a fenced path. With care, cross a level crossing (single track) as the track curves away both to the left and right and continue on a fenced paved path with allotments on the right.

At the end of the allotments (by house No. 3 on the left) fork right over grass to the far right-hand corner. Go ahead with the level crossing on the right over a track and ahead in a narrow field. At a crossing hedge go through the gap and ahead up a steep bank into a playing field.

Continue ahead to a gap about 25 yards to the right of houses on the left and turn left with the hedge on the left. After about 200 yards (where the path turns left into a housing estate) turn right on an unploughed strip. This leads to a clump of trees ahead which surround the remains of a dried up pond where you then turn left on the path leading to a lane by a footpath sign. Turn right and follow the lane round to the left past Rickstones Farm on the right to the main road.

Cross (with extreme care as the road is on a bend with fast traffic) to a signposted green lane opposite. This path (known locally as Kevin's

WALK 22

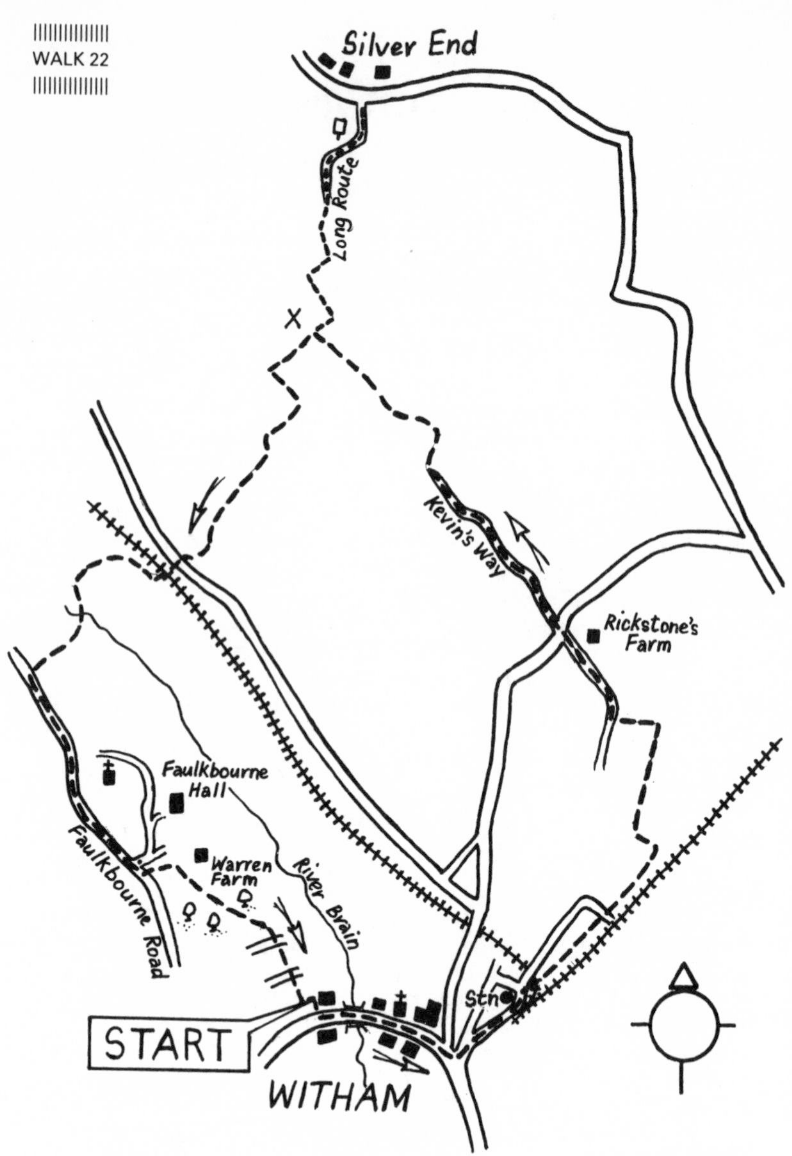

Way) is now truly delightful, going through hedges and trees. It has however required much hard work initially by the Ramblers Association (who first cleared the undergrowth and negotiated with the County Council over the drainage required) and by the County Council who have done later clearance work.

Sadly, as all things must, after about a mile the lane ends in a field. Here turn right with the hedge on your right and in the field corner go through a gap and turn left on a track with the hedge on the left. At a crossing hedge turn right for 25 yards then left on a defined path to a field corner. Continue with the hedge on the left and in a corner go through a gap and continue with the hedge on the left. In the next corner go through a gap onto a wide grassy hedged track (point X). (Note the wood shown ahead at this point on Ordnance Survey maps no longer exists.)

For the longer walk and a visit to the Western Arms see next paragraph, otherwise continue from (**A**) below.

Turn right and at the end of the hedge go left with the hedge on your left. In the corner turn right with the hedge on the left to the end of the hedge. (At this point although I did not find any silver at Silver End if you look ahead to the right you catch a glimpse of silver across the valley as the sun shines on the lakes flanked by the snowy white of the swans guarding the edge of the water.) Turn left on a track over a field. At the corner bear right with the track to turn left over a stile and along a lane to a crossroads with the Western Arms to your left. Return to point X by returning down the lane, over the stile and along the track. In the corner bear left with a track beside power lines. At the top of the hill turn right with the hedge on the right and in the corner go left with the hedge on your right. At the end of the hedge turn right onto a hedged green lane to where the hedge on the left ends (point X).

(**A**) Continue with the hedge on your right to a crossing hedge where you go through a gap and turn left on a track. At a transverse track turn right between a house on your right and a barn on your left to join a hard surfaced track leading ahead out to a road. Turn right for 50 yards then left on a signposted track leading under the railway and past a delightful settlement of houses. The track (stoney) leads ahead then left downhill over the river in the valley by way of ford or bridge. It then leads uphill to a road. Here turn left for about ½ mile walking with care as the road is fairly busy.

You pass Faulkbourne church on your left and beyond it you have outstanding views of the magnificent Faulkbourne Hall. To its right is an unusual clock tower where you can check your watch. Continue past the drive to the hall then turn left on a track with a pillar box to its left and name plate for Warren Farm on its right. You pass Carbonells on your left and just before the entrance to Warren Farm turn right through a gap with the fence on your left. At the end of the fence head half left over a field aiming to join a track on the left where it enters a new plantation. Go ahead on the track between the newly planted trees.

Cross a stile and continue downhill leftish to stiles and a bridge. Continue ahead over a paddock again half left to a stile in the corner to the left of projecting fencing and ahead on a fenced tarmac path. Cross a road and go ahead with the hedge on your left to cross a second road and follow a tarmac path through trees and a grassy area. Just short of the main road (which can be heard ahead) turn left over a bridge and continue on with a hedge on your left. Pass the end of the wall on the left and turn right on the transverse track to the car park.

CURTISMILL GREEN AND MURTHERING LANE

WALK 23

★

4½ miles (7.5 km) or 2½ miles (4 km)

OS Landranger 167/177

Before me as I write lies a press cutting from a London evening newspaper of the early 1930s. The most remote hamlet in England, it would seem, was not deep in a Devon combe or hidden in the Cumbrian fells but only about 17 miles from Central London as the crow flies, and not very far north of the even then rapidly expanding conurbation of Romford and Harold Wood. But the Arcadian retreat — Curtismill Green — had its drawbacks. It was approached only by muddy tracks along which the Faithful had to squelch their way to the nearest church at Stapleford Abbotts and along which the Dear Departed had laboriously to be carried. It was remote from a shop or pub. It was sans gas, electricity or piped water.

Sixty years on, amenities have improved but Curtismill Green has still remained a quiet spot. On my visit I found donkeys and goats tethered there. But its seclusion is now lessened by the M25 which passes just north of it. So, to avoid crossing the motorway I have confined myself to a figure-of-eight route to the south.

Incidentally, I do not know what terrible 'murther' was committed in Murthering Lane. It looked cheerful enough on my visit.

To get to Curtismill Green from London take the A11 to Stratford and then continue to Wanstead. From here take the A113 up the Roding valley through Chigwell and Abridge. Nearly 2 miles beyond Abridge, at a junction where the A113 turns squarely left and the B175 comes in from the right, continue by the minor lane opposite. After about ¾ mile the metalled surface ends at a junction of tracks by a notice 'Curtismill Green. Open to visitors'.

Park discreetly, just off these tracks.

At the fan of tracks at the tarmac end take a look over the gate on the right-hand branch. Beyond is a field but the lodge was once an entrance to Albyns Park. The house has been demolished and a modern farm built on its site. The stable block has, however, survived and the turret on its roof can be seen above the farm buildings in the distance.

To start the walk, take the central track across hummocky grassland, slightly uphill, ignoring branches to properties on the right.

The grassy area through which the track runs widens as it approaches the main green and Green Farm can be seen over to your left. A group of farm buildings is passed a little to your right and then the stoney track has woodland to the left.

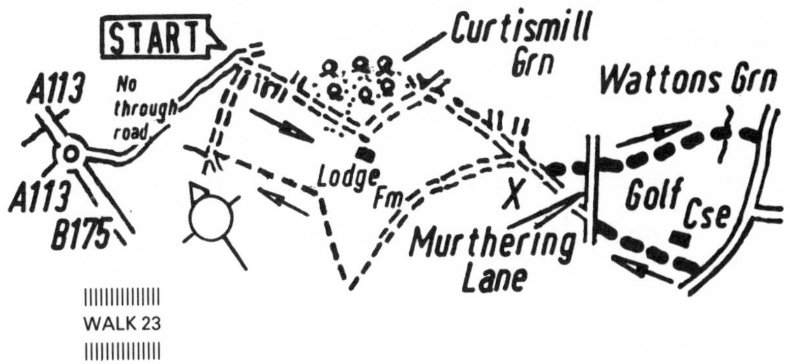

WALK 23

You then approach an unusually shaped house which a nameboard proclaims to be Lodge Farm. Here turn sharp left on a wide dual track. You soon pass Willow Cottage on your right opposite which is an open air theatre where plays by Shakespeare are performed in a fine woodland setting.

Continue ahead and about 20 yards before you reach a gate ahead turn right on a wide track. The route crosses a wooden bridge over the Bourne Brook and (for 300 yards) continues ahead into a fine wide open space surrounded by woodland.

You continue ahead over the grassland to join a drive coming from a house on the left. Follow this drive half right and when the belt of trees on the left ends, turn left onto a path over grassland with trees and a hedge on your left to a further drive.

This is point X where for the shorter walk of 2½ miles you can turn right to a crossing track where you then turn right and continue from (**A**) below. For the main walk, cross the drive and continue ahead to a transverse road (Murthering Lane). Cross over and go along the continuing ride beyond. This green lane was retained when Navestock Common was enclosed. It runs for ¼ mile between bushes. A streamlet is then encountered. If there is any water in it, it can easily be jumped.

Beyond this you enter what appears to be a narrow meadow but which is, in fact, Wattons Green. At its far end you come out on a lane in which you turn rightwards. Ignore, soon, a lane on the left. You then pass, on your right, the entrance to a public golf course.

A little beyond here you come to concrete footpath signs on either side of the road. Go through a hedge gap beside the right-hand one and proceed straight across the golf course to the left of an oak and then keeping a row of trees on your right.

On reaching the far hedge resist the temptation to slant rightwards to a field gate. Instead, *keep straight on* into the corner and there get over wooden bars (I found the erstwhile step missing).

In the small field beyond continue beside the right-hand hedge to a stile at the far end. On my visit I found that the field ahead had been ploughed leaving only a very meagre path but, with the boundary on your right, you do not have to go far until you reach back gardens of houses. Turn rightwards along a narrow enclosed path beyond them. You come out on Murthering Lane again.

Turn rightwards along it for a few yards only and then turn left in the stoney Curtismill Lane which has a timbered cottage on its right and latter-day structure on its left. These, however, are soon left behind.

In 300 yards you come to a triple branch. You have re-reached Point X.

(**A**) Continue ahead over a bridge and carry on slightly uphill passing houses on your right. The track bears round to the left and where it turns sharp right continue ahead into an open space with fine all round views including Epping Forest to the right and Havering water tower to the left.

Continue over the open space with a hedge on the left then go through a gap and on with a wire fence on the right. Halfway along the fence turn right over a meadow to a gate and on with a hedge on the left. You continue through at present three further delightfully grassy meadows with outstanding views keeping the hedge on your left. You then continue over an open field aiming to pass a watertrough on your left (about 10 yards left of an electricity power line pole) and continue leftish to a stile about 20 yards left of the end of the hedge ahead.

Cross and continue ahead over a field soon reaching quite a wide crossing track on which you turn half right aiming to the right of a house in the field corner where you then go through a gate to arrive back at the start of the walk.

BRENTWOOD AND HERONGATE

WALK 24

★

8 miles (13 km)

OS Landranger 177

In the older books one can read nostalgically of Brentwood's coaching era. Present-day Brentwood is very much industrialized but fortunately there is an attractive surrounding green belt which we visit on this walk and where, in the wide open spaces and in the woodlands, factories and tower blocks are completely out of sight and mind.

We go through a part of the Essex County Council's 400-acre Thorndon Country Park, acquired under the green belt scheme in 1939 and designated a country park in 1971. Thorndon has an exceptionally rich natural history and is one of the best sites in Essex to see butterflies. The park is open daily from 8am to dusk. If (and I'm sure you will after a visit) you want to know something of the history of the old Thorndon Hall Estate and the present-day ecological aspects of the country park you can purchase from the information booth at the park itself or from the Essex County Council's Estates Office an illustrated booklet on the subject.

The walk is based on the free car park in Hart's Wood Recreation Ground just south of Brentwood. From central London take the A12(T) to the Brook Street roundabout. Here slant off on the A1023. At the end of Brentwood high street turn rightwards on the Ingrave Road (A128) but quite soon turn right at traffic lights on Seven Arches Road. You will immediately have Shenfield Common on your left.

You cross a railway bridge and come to the Seven Arches pub, the name deriving from the bridge you have just crossed.

A car park sign on the left is now seen practically opposite the inn. Turn left in the approach and so reach the car park.

Continue through the car park and leave through posts by the top left-hand corner. In the recreation ground (King George V Playing Fields) now entered continue on the 'made' path with tennis courts on the right to a broad transverse drive. Here turn left on a path which runs to the left of and parallel to the wide drive. Beyond the municipal golf course car park turn right down a line of trees with the sports field (rugby and cricket in season) on your left and golf course on your right. DO NOT follow the track into the golf course but keep ahead beside and outside it. Go through a gap in the hedge ahead and carry on beside the hedge to the far end of the playing fields. Here turn left towards a house and shortly before reaching it look out for a gap on the right to turn right over a sleeper bridge to a little but busy lane.

Turn left (being careful of passing cars) to the main road (A128).

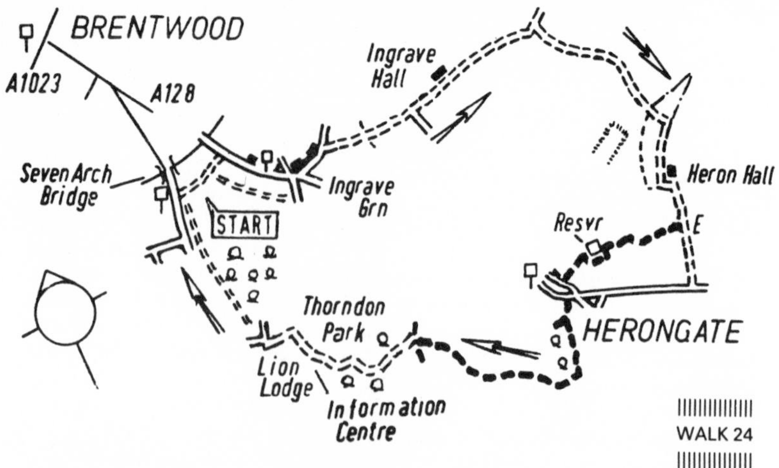

Cross with extreme care and turn right, soon to turn left on a road which bears the rather Hiawatha-like name of Running Waters.

Where, just beyond 'Knightsway' on the left, this road swings left go over a few yards of grass on the right to a signposted bridleway for Ingrave Hall. Immediately inside the field turn left with the hedge and road on your left and shortly, in the field corner, turn right uphill with the hedge on your left. Disregarding a crossing path on the way you come out in about ½ mile to an elbow in a farm road. Here continue forward on a signposted bridleway (No. 72) towards Hutton Hall.

You pass farm buildings and then Ingrave Hall on the left and in about ½ mile beyond the latter (where a line of wood, seen ahead, comes in from the right) you come to a house. Immediately before the entrance to the house turn left and very shortly (immediately before a little bridge) go right on signposted bridleway No. 52 which the signpost indicates leads to Billericay Road. Follow a narrow path with a stream on the left which leads out to a field and then continue along the left edge of the field with the stream still on your left until at the end of the field you cross a transverse stream by a culvert.

The paths around Heron Hall have been officially diverted so if you are following an Ordnance Survey map and the paths shown do not exactly tie in with the following description do not worry as the instructions give the line of the diverted paths.

Turn right to a nearby field corner where you then turn left (slightly uphill) with a wide ditch on your right. Pass a field entrance on the right and opposite farm buildings away to the right the track turns right over a bridge to pass to the left-hand side of these buildings. Beyond a barn turn right on a track to join a farm road coming out of Heron Hall. Turn left on this farm road towards housing seen ahead.

Halfway towards these houses (by the first ditch on the right) turn right on a signposted footpath indicating the way to Billericay Road and Cricketers Lane. Crossing bridges and keeping the ditch on your left you have on your right a good view of the mellow old Heron Hall. When the hedge on your left ends continue ahead over a field to a stile near the left-hand edge of a reservoir bank. Cross the stile and turn left. (BE CAREFUL of a hole in the path by a manhole as soon as you turn left.) The path soon turns right and at the far end of the reservoir right again to come out by a white cottage at the waterworks drive. Turn left in this and at a T-junction (Cricketers Lane with its picturesque houses), left again to the Green Man pub (4½ miles from the start).

Opposite the Green Man turn right to the main road (A128). Cross with care to Park Lane and when it almost immediately turns left go ahead over grass through guard posts to turn leftwards on a path. Proceed now by the obvious path downhill through scrub and clumps of trees coming out to an outstanding view away to your left. After about ½ mile you reach the entrance to Thorndon Country Park. Go through a gap and turn right onto a signposted path to West Horndon which runs just inside the right edge of woodland, with glimpses of a golf course away to your right. The path drops steeply to cross a stream and then rises just as steeply. Near the top of the rise be careful to look out for, and turn right on, a signposted footpath.

The path runs on beside the golf course for about ¾ mile. There are again outstanding views to the left and as you approach the end of the path you get a sighting of the first of the trees planted on the new Thames Chase Community Forest. This is the start of an exciting project to create a 35 mile forest for east London but judging by the number of trees planted so far this looks like being a very long term project.

At the end of the path turn left through bars to very soon meet a transverse drive where you can either turn right on the drive or more pleasantly cross it and turn right in the trees beside it. There are any number of paths which can be followed as long as you do not wander too far from the made up drive.

You pass a car park and shortly come to a second car park. Here there are toilets and the information centre which is open daily from 10am to 5pm in summer and 10am to 3.30pm in winter (except Mondays). This is a joint venture between the Essex County Council and the Essex Wildlife Trust. The building is constructed from timber salvaged from the 1987 storm. It is well worth a visit for its informative displays, school room with working exhibits, gift shop and not least its excellent coffee.

From the centre continue ahead to pass through the trim Lion Gates and bear right to the road. Cross to a path opposite into woodland. At a fork bear right continuing with the boundary fence on your right. After crossing bridges you come to a crossing track where you then turn right and almost immediately left. Fork left on a footpath ignoring paths to the right and left. The path bears right to rejoin a parallel bridleway and continues ahead over a main crossing path. Beyond here cross a bridge and turn left. At a fork keep left over a crossing track and continue ahead back into the playing fields. Pass between the putting green and children's playground to a crossing track. Cross leftish to continue with the tennis courts to your right and fork right over a circular paved area into magnificent gardens. There are seats from which to admire the flowers before turning right, back into the car park.

EAST HORNDON (THORNDON PARK SOUTH), CHILDERDITCH STREET AND JURY HILL

WALK 25

★

3 or 5 miles (5 or 8 km)

OS Landranger 177

This walk is complementary to Walk 24 as it goes over another — the southern — part of Thorndon Country Park. Indeed, the two walks can be linked to give a 13 mile walk, but most visitors will doubtless prefer a shorter walk as here indicated, the better to explore the fine park at leisure. Enjoy its fine woodlands, lakes, open country and the wide views — a little industrialized in the distance, perhaps, but very rural in the foreground.

To Thorndon Park take the A12(T) from Wanstead to Gallows Corner keeping in right-hand lane over the flyover for the A127. Follow for about 6 miles to East Horndon and then turn left on the A128 (Brentwood) road. After about 200 yards turn left on a signposted lane to Thorndon Country Park and immediately fork right on to a turning leading to the car park. This car park is free in winter but a charge is made at weekends in summer. (Car park closes in evening so watch out for any notices about closing time before starting the walk.)

Continue to the end of the car park (walking on the grass beside it) and here continue ahead on the track past the notice board which bears a plan of the park on it. Continue with the track through a small wood, past toilets on the left and on, downhill, with good all-round views, towards a second wood. Continue on through this (ignoring tracks to right) and again forward to the lake.

A few yards short of the lake turn rightwards over an earth bridge and keep on the track (rather more grassy at this point) with the lake to your left. The track continues uphill through rather open woodland at first and gradually veers away (rightwards) from the lake (Old Hall Pond) and continues on the right-hand edge of a wood and with a valley on your left for ½ mile.

At the end of the wood turn left on a footpath signposted for Childerditch Street (and a quaint variation of Horndon as 'Hordon') at the right edge of woodland. Here you are briefly on Walk 24 which can be combined with this walk to give a walk of up to 13 miles. Follow the path through a dip with a golf course, and later a field, on the right. Ignore paths to left and right and continue on the edge of the wood (which later becomes mainly coniferous). Towards the end of the conifers the path bears rightwards and continues on a field edge to a

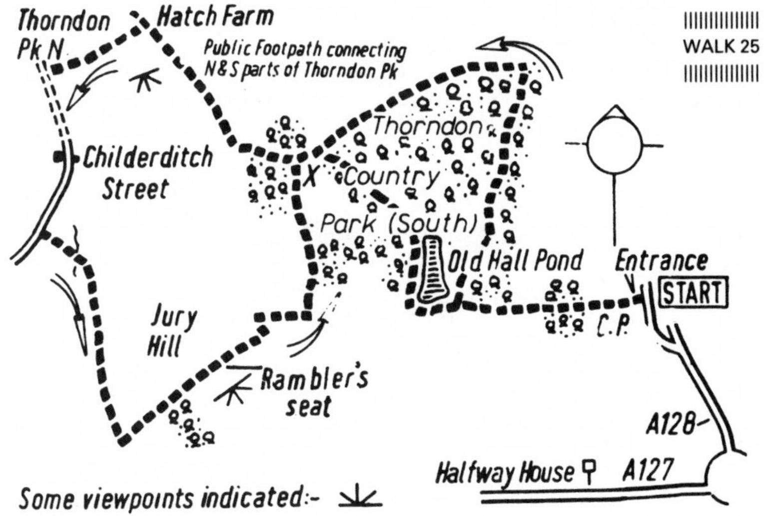

signposted footpath junction — point X. (For the shorter walk turn *left* into the edge of a wood and see note which follows.)

For the main walk turn half right on a narrow path (signposted for Childerditch Street) uphill into woodland and follow, currently over one or two fallen trees, over a rough area and out into a field. Continue on the right-hand edge of the field uphill to a crossing track.

Turn right on this signposted track for just over ¼ mile and just short of Hatch Farm ahead turn left (by an electricity pole) on a footpath signposted for Childerditch Street. Here pause to admire the view over the Thames basin and the Kent Hills to the south and to Childerditch ahead. The clear path runs downhill later with a ditch on the left and in the valley crosses a bridge to go right and left over a stile by a gate and a notice about Thorndon Park byelaws.

Turn left and follow the track between the scattered houses which make up Childerditch Street. After about ¼ mile on a made-up lane by a house on the left (Meadow View) go ahead for a few yards and then turn left on a footpath signposted to West Horndon. Go ahead to a stile opposite. Cross an earth bridge and turn right with a brook on your right.

Go over a stile in the field corner and continue with a hedge on your right. Midway down the field (by a gate on the right where a track comes in from the right) go half left uphill on a narrow path to and through the left-hand of two gates in the far left-hand corner of the field. Follow the hedge on the right with steeply rising ground to the left to a stile by a footpath sign.

Do not cross the stile but turn round with your back to it. Here head diagonally (half right) in the direction of a signpost to Herongate, uphill. You are aiming for a stile in a field corner on the right-hand side of the crown of the rise (Jury Hill) in this field. Cross by a footpath sign and turn rightwards with a ditch on your right. This is the high spot of the walk and is where the Brentwood Group of the Ramblers Association have erected a seat in commemoration of the 21st Anniversary of the founding of the group. This gives you and the many other walkers who use this well trodden route a chance to rest awhile and enjoy one of the really outstanding views of Essex before continuing back to the country park.

At the field corner turn left for 100 yards then rightwards into a crossing track by a footpath signpost. Turn rightwards for 10 yards and then left on a signposted footpath with ditch and hedge on the right. When the hedge turns sharp right, turn left on a signposted path across a field (uphill) aiming for the far left-hand edge of a wood. (Note the rear views.) Continue with the wood on your right past a footpath sign and on along a path across a field towards a further wood.

Keep ahead with woodland on the left bearing rightwards with it to a signposted footpath junction in a dip. Go ahead past a signpost (for Herongate) and almost immediately turn rightwards on a narrow path into the edge of a wood.

This is where those doing the shorter walk join in.

Follow the path which meanders gradually leftwards but keeps near the *right* edge of the wood. Soon there is a stream on your right. This is a very pleasant woodland path, mainly on the stream bank, with birdsong to enliven your way. After about ¼ mile the woodland becomes more open as you keep ahead. As the lake in the valley becomes visible you bear rightwards over a rather marshy area and follow along the right-hand side of the lake.

This is a delightful spot. At the end of the lake turn left with the lake on your left and retrace the outward route along the wide track ahead uphill into woodland and back to the car park.

CHINGFORD AND GILWELL PARK

WALK 26

★

6 miles (9.5 km)

OS Landranger 177

I have been out of touch with scouting for some time now so I do not know whether, nowadays, they sing rousing songs around a camp fire at the end of the day. But as I walked up the drive leading to Gilwell Park, the famous scout camp and training ground, I found myself humming 'I used to be a 'pecker . . .' and promising myself to get back to 'Gilwell, Happy Land. I'm gonna work my ticket if I can'.

There are some good views on this walk, one being as good as, and in much quieter surroundings, than the better-known prospect at High Beach (see Walk 27).

One word of caution is that in winter months or after prolonged wet weather it is advisable to wear 'wellies' on this walk as although most if not all muddy patches can be avoided by walking in the trees beside the paths, there can be muddy sections after heavy rain.

Park opposite the Royal Forest Hotel up the hill on Rangers Road, ¼ mile east of Chingford station. This is a 'trust' car park with a collection box for parking fees, no tickets are issued, the money collected going towards the upkeep of the forest.

If starting from Chingford station forecourt go rightwards, down to the main road. Here turn rightwards in Forest Avenue (continued as the Rangers Road) soon to reach the Hunting Lodge. From the other car park you merely cross the road to the Hunting Lodge.

Immediately beyond the refreshment house (Butler's Retreat, one of a number of such retreats or refreshment houses in the forest which were popular in the period between the two World Wars) which follows the Hunting Lodge, turn in, left, to the tall, now non-functional, drinking fountain. From the drinking fountain turn half right on a clear downward sloping path between ditches and occasional white posts (indicating this is a horse ride). Presently another track joins from the right and the route bends a little left over a culvert to enter the forest as a broad gravelled ride.

A transverse ride is crossed and soon another joins from the right. Continue ahead. A transverse ride is crossed and soon a reedy pool is seen on the right. (Ignore a number of casual horse tracks which join this main surfaced ride from left and right and keep straight on.)

After ¼ mile a major ride joins from the left followed quickly by a fork. Take the left-hand branch, which promptly crosses another ride. Keep ahead for a further ½ mile to where the ride bends left then swings right with grassy tracks joining from left and right. Hereabouts

the Metropolitan Police communications masts may be seen away to the left across a grassy area. Our ride now makes a sharp right turn followed after a few yards by a sharp left turn. The ride now climbs steeply uphill, entering the wood again. Eventually it reaches the crest and more level ground. (All along this section can be seen the gaunt remains of many fine beech trees which were uprooted, or otherwise severely damaged during the storm of October 1987.)

Eventually the road is reached, where junctions can be seen both to the right and left. A refreshment hut is usually to be found at the right-hand junction, but to continue the walk turn left and subsequently fork left on a traffic carrying road. For some of the way along the road which can be busy at times, you will find it possible to walk on a parallel path just inside the forest on the left. On the way look out on the right for High Beach church, a delightful church surrounded by the trees of the forest.

Continue to the crossroads where you then turn left until a Y-junction is reached. Take the right-hand Mott Street branch past pillared Wallsgrove House. The top of a 1:8 gradient hill is reached with a nice view over a paddock to the right.

Now turn left along a drive named Pepper Alley. At the end of this you come to three gates. Take the central white-painted metal one which leads you on to a hedged path, which in turn brings you through a gate to a field.

Before continuing the basic walk a slight detour for a really good viewpoint is recommended. For this, turn rightwards past a holly bush to a stile (point X). Over this continue over the next field (hedge on right) to another stile — and here's your view. Return to point X and follow the power line path. This will be half left of your original approach.

The grassy path brings you to another (rather dilapidated) gate, followed by a further section of enclosed path, a part of which is nearly always badly churned up by horses' hooves. The path leads out past a pond on the right to a lane with the Owl pub to your left. Turn right and after about 100 yards where the houses on the left end, turn left on a signposted bridleway alongside a golf course. A fine view soon opens up on the right with the abbey church of Waltham Abbey soon coming into sight. The distant traffic on the M25 will also be evident.

A little way along on the left is a memorial to a World War II United States Aircraft Unit which was based here. The path in time makes a left-hand bend with the hedge then soon makes a right-hand bend to a signpost. Turn left here in the direction of Sewardstonebury with the hedge on the left. At the corner of the hedge with the magnificent turkey oaks ahead turn left with the hedge still on your left, downhill to join the drive from the palatial new clubhouse of the West Essex Golf Club. Turn right along the driveway, but please remember that it crosses the fairway and keep a look out for possible golf balls coming your way.

The drive brings you out onto a road where you then turn left for a couple of hundred yards, then turn right along the drive to Gilwell Park which is so signposted. On reaching the impressive main gate of the famous scout camp turn left on the transverse track. Where the made-up surface ends continue on a grassy track. This soon turns right but you continue ahead to a stile beside a metal gate. Beyond the stile turn right with trees on your right. This lovely open area, Yates Meadow, is a recent addition to Epping Forest and is a picture of colour in spring and summer months when flowers are in bloom.

But the attraction is not only underfoot for there is an excellent view to be had from the hill we are now ascending. In the middle distance is what appears to be an inland sea (in reality Thames Water's enormous William Girling Reservoir). Beyond, on the skyline, you will be able to make out the outline of Alexandra Palace with its mast. It was from there that the BBC broadcast the first public TV service back in 1936. Further to the left you will be able to glimpse many of the taller buildings of central London, and in the foreground over the valley the wooded slope of Pole Hill, magnificent at all times but especially so in late October and November with the blaze of autumn colours.

Back to the walk: keep beside the trees on your right round the top of the meadow and in the corner turn left downhill beside trees on your right. At the bottom of the hill you reach a small but obvious gap on the right and passing through turn left for 20 yards or so then left again on a made-up horse ride. The ride climbs gradually through delightful woodland and after ½ mile reaches a road. Cross it and turn right parallel to the road on the adjacent horse ride. Ignore the two rides entering the forest on your left and emerge onto the open grassland of Chingford Plain. Turn left along the edge of the trees to shortly reach a horse trough on your left. Here turn right on a path across the plain over a bridge and on uphill to the back of Butler's Retreat and the Hunting Lodge, back to the car park.

HIGH BEACH AND EPPING FOREST

WALK 27

★

7 miles (11 km)

OS Landranger 166, 167, 177

Perhaps High Beach with its car park is a little too popular. But the view from this, the crown of Epping Forest, is magnificent. Westward it extends country-into-town over Enfield Chase and Waltham Abbey is seen below. Tennyson (who came to live nearby) got the inspiration for his famous lines 'Ring out, wild bells . . .' from hearing the abbey chimes.

Whilst there are many visitors who never get out of their cars, others sniff appreciatively and declare they can detect the tang of the sea blowing in from over the Thames estuary. And there are the *Beach v Beech* protagonists. The consensus of opinion (backed by the Ordnance Survey) would have it (as I do) that it is *beach* (ie a gravel bank) though admittedly there are many beech trees hereabouts.

According to popular legend Ambersbury Banks (which we traverse) was the spot from which Boadicea, gallant Queen of the Iceni, set out westward to fight her last battle against the all-conquering Romans. This bit of pop-history has been dismissed as fanciful. The banks are, the learned men say, an Iron Age earthwork constructed between 300 BC and AD 100.

There are many more modern minded, however, who are interested in the defence works thrown up in the forest during World War II. Some of these have been retained for their historic interest. On this present walk we can see them on the lane from the Copped Hall Lodge gates down to the B1393, through Ambersbury Banks and along the Ditches Ride.

If you have time, and if it is open, a visit to the Epping Forest Conservation Centre is well worthwhile.

Probably the best way to High Beach is to make for the Wake Arms — the focal point of the forest roads, shown on all touring maps, and then take the road signposted for High Beach. Park in the car park at High Beach.

At High Beach face the view and then turn rightwards past the tea hut which is on your left. Beyond the tea hut enter the forest on a track running parallel to the road on your right. At a transverse road, cross the road (to the left of the road junction) and continue ahead in the forest beside a fairly recently constructed horse ride (which is on the line of the 'Verderer's Ride'). Follow for its full length, ignoring a left fork and keeping on top of the ridge. This leads out to the main road almost opposite Woodredon Farm Lane. Cross with care (leftish) and follow this lane ahead, bearing rightwards on the metalled surface, to pass

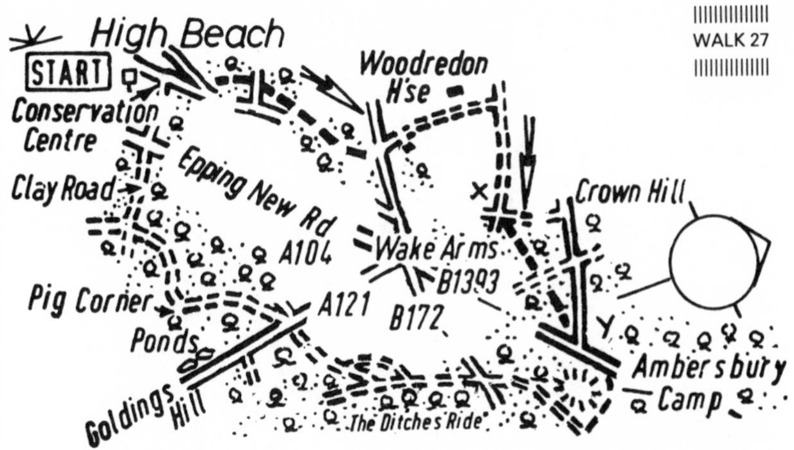

through lodge gates with a charming duckpond on your right. Continue ahead.

There is soon a very fine town-country view on the left and then a forest façade one on the right. You subsequently pass Woodredon House on the left. On reaching a T-junction turn rightwards.

You are now on a rough but very beautiful little hedged green lane. It subsequently veers a trifle rightwards and narrows a lot.

Since I first knew it the lovely woodland track which follows has been cleared somewhat and on my survey visit I found it easy to avoid inevitable muddy parts. You emerge through gate posts (the gate has long since gone) on that part of Epping Forest known as St Thomas's Quarters.

Here (point X) you can do one of two things:

(a) Turn leftwards on a track with the forest boundary to your left. Subsequently make a leftward turn to pass a house (Poachers' Meet) over to your left and so emerge on the road at Crown Hill. Here turn rightwards and follow out, passing the impressive gates of Copped Hall (and disregarding a turning opposite) to reach the Epping New Road (point Y).

(b) If, like myself, you remember with affection your scouting days and still fancy yourself as a backwoodsman (or as Peggy The Peerless Pathfinder) *and have taken a pocket compass along* strike off north-eastwards from point X. No marked path shows through the trees (chiefly beech) but there is plenty of room to manoeuvre. There is not much undergrowth but you may have to detour round patches of holly. You cross a lane (and see the gates of Copped Hall to the left along it) and continue your adventurous nor'-east way until by lucky chance or dead reckoning you arrive (well, more or less!) at point Y. You will probably arrive on the lane just short of this and then turn rightwards.

Either way: Cross the main road (when you are able) and turn left for a short way until you reach an iron 'coal post'.

There was once an Act of Parliament which gave the Corporation of

London the right to levy a duty on all coals entering the metropolis. In 1861 iron posts were set up to define the perimeter of the toll area. The duty no longer applies, but a large number of coal posts remain and can be 'collected' photographically. Here's one to start with!

Keep ahead past the coal post with Ambersbury Banks on your right. This was a camp of the Ancient Britons and although time has blunted the mounds and part-filled the hollows, the earthworks are still impressive. At the end of the earthworks turn right on a narrow path leading directly away from the road until you come to an absolutely unmistakable transverse riders' track, fairly wide and gravelled. Turn rightwards in this. Now that it is semi-'made' it offers fairly easy going as most soft parts can easily be sidetracked. This is The Green Road. It is to the forest tracks what the Epping New Road is to the forest highways.

On reaching a transverse road cross over and continue, now on that part of the Green Road called The Ditches Ride, at first gravelled and sanded. After ½ mile, fork right and follow a track to the main road. Cross with extreme care onto a continuing track leading ahead (leftish). It brings you, in ½ mile or so, to a distinct bend (Pig Corner — the meeting place of several streams). A little beyond this disregard the Y-shaped double head of a right-hand track. A hundred yards past this, however, turn rightwards on a *transverse* track. You are now on the Clay Road named not from its subsoil but from a mid-Victorian property developer who, before the forest was secured for the public, hoped to line it with houses.

On reaching the Epping New Road cross over and follow the path/track until your forward way is stopped by a fence. Here turn right-left and so, past the Epping Forest Conservation Centre (as already hinted, well worth a visit) and over two roads, come back to your starting point.

HADLEIGH CASTLE COUNTRY PARK, BENFLEET AND LEIGH-ON-SEA

WALK 28

★

4, 8 or 9 miles (6.4, 12.4 or 15.2 km)

OS Landranger 178

The present walk brings a breath of the briny into this book; if not the open sea then at least the creek country of the Thames estuary and places where they mess about in boats.

Given a bright day with, preferably, a 'busy' sky (this area could be rather cheerless on a dull day) you will find the saltings and the marshes (the latter being green pastures and not normally swamps) of considerable charm and interest. Even the most amateur of botanists armed with a simple plant-identification book will delight in looking for such maritime plants as the horned poppy, sea rocket, sea kale and many, many more. You will have a chance to visit a nature reserve and if you are not a naturalist yourself you may possibly (like myself) find the visiting naturalists interesting.

But the highspot (literally and metaphorically) of this walk is Hadleigh Castle. It was originally built by Hubert de Burgh in 1230 and Edward I gave it to his queen. It was rebuilt in 1365 and, later, another king — Henry VIII — gave it to his queen, the unwanted Anne of Cleves.

From the castle ruins is a wonderful map-like view over the Thames estuary across to the blue hills of Kent. The striking ruins of Hadleigh Castle formed the subject of one of John Constable's pictures (1829). The painting is now in the Tate Gallery. The actuality is there for you to enjoy.

The walk is based on the Hadleigh Castle Country Park where there is a car park in Chapel Lane. All routes visit Hadleigh Castle and the 9 mile walk includes the exploration of Two Tree Island (a very worthwhile extension if time permits).

To reach this take the A13 to Hadleigh and then follow road signs to the country park car park in Chapel Lane. Alternatively the walk can be started (mainly at weekends and on bank holidays) from either Leigh-on-Sea or Benfleet stations, but car parking is difficult, if not impossible, at these stations on weekdays due to their use by commuters on the busy Fenchurch Street Line.

From the car park (where there are toilets) go through the kissing gate by the information boards and map of the country park. Turn left and follow the fenced path down some steps and through another kissing gate to a large open space with excellent views downhill over the Thames estuary. As you descend the hill gradually make your way to the right

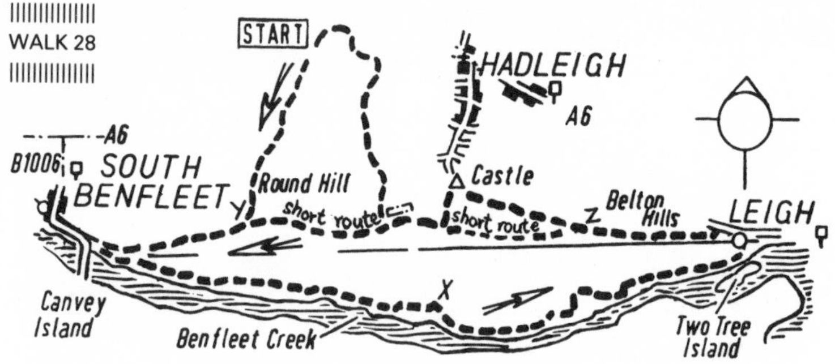

and follow the hedge until you come to a gate and stile (ignoring stiles and paths off to the right). Cross the stile and the new horse ride to turn right over another stile and then immediately left through woods following a stream down the hill. (At the bottom of the hill (point Y) the routes divide. For main route see (**A**) below.)

For the short route do not cross the stile on the right but turn left along the edge of the wood and scrubland on your left and with the railway away to your right. Beyond the woodland you pass a path leading left up Sandpit Hill (used on the return route) and later a path also on your left leading up to Hadleigh Castle. Continue ahead passing below the castle to where a third path (the main path to Hadleigh Castle) comes in from the left (point Z). Turn left and continue from (**B**) below.

(**A**) For the main walk turn right to the bottom of the hill over a stile and follow the path until you reach a gate and stile by a small pond. Crossing the stile you will see a gate that reads 'Kersey and Poynets' and carries the country park logo. Continue in the same direction with the railway on your left over stiles until you come to a metal gate and a stile close to the railway with a clear cinder path.

At the fingerpost cross the railway *with extreme care* (Benfleet station will be to your right). Another stile leads on to a metalled road with the bridge to Canvey Island to your right. Turn left along a track towards Benfleet Creek where you will see an armada of boats including some houseboats. Pass a Thames barrier (not the London one) on your right and follow the creek to cross a stile by the wooden gate carrying the park logo. The footpath is just below the top of the seawall to its right and is at first a cinder path but soon becomes grassy. From here there are fine views across the railway to the tree covered slopes of the country park and in the distance Hadleigh Castle and St Clement's church at Leigh-on-Sea.

It is difficult, if not impossible to get lost along here as you follow the path until you reach a stile and metal gate. From the top of the seawall at this point (point X), you should see the remains of a red brick bridge which was used in the transportation of bricks but more about this later, and at the top of the hill, The Salvation Army Home Farm.

Cross the stile ahead by a gate and continue along the creek. On your right you will shortly pass the remains of a wharf where the bricks (mentioned earlier) from the brickworks ½ mile distant were unloaded onto barges. A short distance after this looking across the creek you should notice a stile.

Look for the causeway across the creek leading to this stile and onto Two Tree Island. Here the walk could be extended to take in an exploration of the island and its nature reserve. Note however that *the causeway can only be crossed at low tide* and is muddy on the surface but quite firm underneath as it has been built up with rocks and stones. If the causeway is covered and unwalkable but you still want to visit the island it can be reached by continuing ahead to the road bridge and turning right on to the island. Hopefully however the causeway is available and you can cross the stile.

To the right of the stile is a lagoon and public bird hide from where many interesting birds can be seen. In this direction you can walk round the seaward side of the island which adds about ½ mile to the walk. On reaching the road and slipway follow the road until you cross the bridge off the island to rejoin the main walk.

If not visiting Two Tree Island continue alongside the sea wall until a transverse road is reached by the bridge leading to the island. About 50 yards to your left down the road is a golf driving range where tea, coffee and other light refreshments can be obtained, but our walk continues over the road and on along the sea wall with playing fields on your left.

When the sea wall ends you find yourself on the road to Leigh-on-Sea station. A turning on the right will take you into Old Leigh past the famous cockle sheds and public houses and teashops but our route passes over the railway and turns left past the station. Continue along the road until Castle Drive is reached where you then turn left and continue to the end of the road and over a stile onto a crossfield path. This leads to a scrub covered area and a sign which reads 'Belton Hills'. Follow the wide grassy path between hedges and then the field edge path with a fence on the right to a stile (point Z).

(**B**) Now climb the whaleback ridge to the remains of Hadleigh Castle, and enjoy the fine views over the estuary. You reach the perimeter railings of the castle, cross a stile and follow the railings on your left. At the corner of the railings turn left where there is a gate for entry to the ruins. After looking around and again enjoying the view, you have to leave by the same gate and cross the stile beside it to the wide track leading downhill. The footpath does not follow this track but leaves it and heads diagonally to a stile in the far corner at the bottom of the hill. Follow the field edge path with a fence on the right. The brickworks mentioned previously used to be around here but nothing now remains except perhaps the odd brick in the soil. Continue ahead to cross a stile with a fingerpost to your left.

Follow the direction indicated up the hill crossing stiles and following clear waymarks on posts. At the top of the hill pass to the right of a brick building to a stile in the left-hand corner of a pasture onto a track. Turn left with a reservoir on your left hidden behind high banks. At the T-junction turn right and you will see the path into the car park on your left.

SOUTH WEALD COUNTRY PARK (BRENTWOOD), NAVESTOCK SIDE AND PILGRIMS HATCH

WALK 29

★

4, 6 or 8 miles (6.5, 9.5 or 13 km)

OS Landranger 177

Thorndon Country Park is visited in Walks 24 and 25. This walk introduces you to Brentwood's other country park, South Weald — a delightful domain of undulating parkland, woodland and lakes, with such amenities as picnic areas. There are also fine views. Industrial Brentwood is indeed fortunate in having two fine country parks so close to hand. The choice of mileage enables one readily to adapt the walk if one wishes to explore the park further or if one is tempted to linger to watch village cricket being played adjacent to the country pub at Navestock Side.

It is hoped, however, that adventurous readers will do the full round either on one visit or do 'left-out' sections on a further visit. The green lanes here, as elsewhere, can be somewhat wet after a prolonged rainy season but they are very rewarding during the drier season.

To arrive at the starting point follow the A12(T) from Wanstead to Brentwood, being careful to take the slip-road off the start of the dual carriageway (for Brentwood). Approximately ½ mile beyond the roundabout turn left in Wiggley Bush Lane and follow it to South Weald. At the T-junction turn left, downhill. Do not enter the car park on the right but continue with Weald Park on the right, past the lakes. At the next fork veer right (Lincoln's Lane) — this is a narrow road with bends, so caution is needed. After ¼ mile or so you will find a car park on the right. This is the one to use. Parking here is free during the week but at weekends during the summer season a charge is made.

From the far side of the car park follow a track left (parallel to Lincoln's Lane) uphill. This gradually bears to the right and gives excellent views over to South Weald church and also to the lakes below. Keep to this ridge track eventually reaching some wooden gates (½ mile from the start). A dozen yards or so beyond these turn left on a track with conifers on your right. After ½ mile you cross a stile by the park boundary gates, passing on your left a house called 'Badgers Cottage' and keeping ahead to the road.

Cross the road slightly left to pass through kissing gates on the signposted footpath for Bentley. Cross a meadow to the stile ahead then continue over a second meadow to a bridge and stile. Here head half left to a stile in a gap in the trees and beyond the stile carry on with a hedge

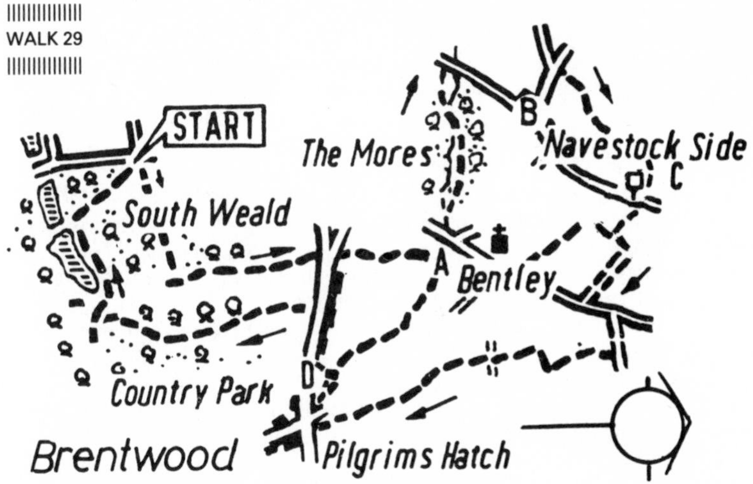

on your right. Continue in the same direction across two further stiles arriving at a crossing track (point A).

(For the 4 mile walk turn right here and see notes at end.)

For the full round you turn left, soon reaching a lane. Cross over to Snakes Lane where you will see a signpost for Wheeler's Lane (¾ mile). Take this path which runs roughly parallel with the left-hand edge of the wood, passing farm buildings on the left. Ignore a waymarked path to the right and continue straight on. Eventually, at two large storm damaged beech trees, the path veers leftwards, confirmed shortly afterwards by a waymark. A new fishing lake will be seen across the fence on the left. Soon marshy ground and a stream are crossed with the aid of duckboards. Be careful as they could be slippery after rain.

The path now veers to the right and continues with the stream on the right. Keep ahead ignoring a branch path going to the right. The left-hand edge of the wood should always remain just about visible. Two further bridges are crossed before the path emerges from the wood onto the road by a house called Pantile Hall. Turn right along the road for about 600 yards until the junction with Princes Road is reached (point B).

Here you have an option. Our next objective is the Green Man pub at Navestock Side which can be reached either by lane, about ½ mile distant simply by continuing ahead along the road, or the footpath way, which will reward you with fine views.

For this turn left along Princes Road and in a short ¼ mile (immediately before a road junction on the left) turn right over a stile. Cross the field parallel to the field edge, aiming for a large oak tree on the far side. Pass to the right of this single oak and continue with a hedge on the right to a stile in a hedge by a further large oak tree. Cross and head diagonally left to a second stile 30 yards away across a grassy strip. Here head upwards across a field aiming for a wide gap at the left-hand edge of a belt of trees on a ridge with the Green Man pub visible beyond them to the right. As you climb the field you get a fine view of a large house called Dudbrook away over the fields ahead. At the top of the field turn right on a track passing through a gap to continue with the hedge on your right along a track to emerge beside the Green Man pub.

Here is a good opportunity for refreshments, and at appropriate times, the chance to watch village cricket in a truly rural setting.

Here (point C) is the branching off point for the 6 mile walk — see note at end.

For the full route. With your back to the pub, turn left on the road and quite soon turn rightwards on a metalled track behind the cricket pavilion. This soon brings you to another lane in which you turn left for a couple of hundred yards and then, at a lane junction, turn squarely rightwards on what is at first a green lane but which subsequently, with houses on its left, acquires a 'made' surface. At Old Crown Lane it is followed out to the main road where you then turn left for about 250 yards then cross to, and turn along, a path signposted 'Byway no 7'. This passes in front of the clubhouse of Bentley golf course.

After ¼ mile in this direction, and at a clump of bushes running ahead, turn squarely rightwards on a rather faint path running across the fairway (look both ways before you cross!). Another clue to identifying the spot where you turn is that at this point a series of short white posts commences running in your original direction. The new path soon becomes obvious on the ground as it passes a green and drops down to cross an earth bridge before veering left and climbing a steady rise between bushes.

At the crest, where it emerges into the open again, the path curves to the right as a cinder track for a brief period. Very quickly it leaves the cinder track by forking left through bushes. (This short section might well, in wet weather, be chewed up by horses' hooves.)

The path soon reaches a gate where you turn left, with buildings on your right, and so out to a road. Cross over and continue by a path opposite for about ¾ mile, dead straight, ignoring paths and tracks coming in from the left. Eventually you reach Gent's Farm on the left. Here continue ahead passing through two sets of metal barriers whereafter the path becomes first a track and then a metalled lane which emerges rightwards onto the main road. Cross with care to a junction almost opposite.

The route we want is just to the right of Coxtie Green Road and almost parallel to it; a track with a No Through Road sign. This soon becomes a path and after ¼ mile when the end of a metalled road meets the path, turn left along this road with housing to the left. The road soon joins the main Coxtie Green Road (point D).

All walks now follow the same route. Here turn right past a large Pentecostal school and continue on until you reach a track on the left opposite a house, No. 63. This track leads to a stile giving re-entry to Weald Park, passing on the way giant heating ducts for the modern greenhouses on either side.

Cross the stile and keep straight on (ignoring paths coming in from left and right) and going gradually downhill. Near the bottom of the dip ignore a left fork leading over a rise. Instead bear sharp right with the track and with a seat on the left for a welcome rest. Cross an earth bridge and follow on up a sharp rise. Near the top turn half left with the track, through bracken and scattered oaks and out into a wide avenue of chestnut trees.

Turn left, downhill with a charming view ahead. Just short of the gates at the end of the avenue turn rightwards on a track towards the lake. Keep on beside the lake (water on left) and when a path goes off leftwards to a bridge between the two lakes turn *rightwards* on a path going uphill over the grass. In a couple of hundred yards you pass a pond on your right and then turn left on a path leading from a convenient establishment on the right. When this path veers a little to the left go half right, uphill, on a path over grass aiming for the left of a house seen ahead, and so back to the car park.

Note for the 4-mile walk

At point A turn *rightwards* and follow the track for about ½ mile until, 100 yards after passing a black weatherboard house (The Cottage) you can turn rightwards, on a metalled road with houses on the left, to the main road (point D). Now return to the main text and follow directions from *'All walks now follow the same route.'*

Note for the 6-mile walk

From the Green Man at Navestock Side (point C) turn left for a very short distance and then follow a metalled track behind the cricket pavilion which runs into a lane in which you turn right for a couple of hundred yards or so. Then take a signposted path on the left. This runs south-east along the right-hand side of a hedge and then over a bridge. In the second field maintain your direction passing by the right-hand side of the near oak tree. (A waymark confirms the direction.) Cross a stile on the far side and go down a short track out to meet a three-way road junction. Take the rightmost (minor one) of these, soon passing a left-hand and then a right-hand turn. Bentley church is then passed and you reach a point where a road slants in from the right.

Here turn left on a signposted track. Follow this byway for about ½ mile and 100 yards after passing a black weatherboard house (The Cottage) turn rightwards on a metalled road with housing on its left out to the main road (point D). Now return to the main text and follow directions from *'All walks now follow the same route.'*

STOCK, RIVER WID AND MARGARETTING CHURCH

WALK 30

★

8 miles (13 km)

OS Landranger 167/177

This walk is based on the delightful village of Stock with its views from its hillside position between Chelmsford and Billericay. Stock windmill visited on this walk is one of a number which are now owned and maintained by the Essex County Council. It is of the tower variety, where the cap could be rotated on metal runners so that the sails would point into the prevailing wind, as differentiated from the post variety where the body of the mill revolved with the sails round a central post. An example of a post mill can be seen at Mountnessing on the way from London to Stock.

The walk, which is one of fine tracks and wide views, starts from the church with its impressive wooden tower — one of the most delightful in Essex — and spire which are of the same type as those of Blackmore and Margaretting. The latter in its fine isolated setting is passed on this walk; Blackmore is visited on Walk 17.

To reach Stock take the A12(T) from Wanstead and keep on when it becomes the Brentwood bypass. Then take the first exit (for Mountnessing and Ingatestone (B1002). Follow into Ingatestone and almost immediately after passing the church on your right turn right on a narrow lane for Stock. Be careful at the narrow turn into this lane and also at the hump-back bridge about 1 mile down the lane. The bridge is restricted to single lane traffic so watch out for oncoming traffic on your approach to it.

The road bears right to the lonely Buttsbury church and then left. After a further 2 miles turn left for Stock. After ¼ mile turn left with care onto the B1007 into Stock.

Park discreetly in the village.

Enter the churchyard and at its end go half right on a narrow paved path and then on with a hedge on your left and the churchyard on your right. Go through a gate and on with the hedge on your left into a dip where you cross a bridge and proceed uphill with a hedge still on your left. At the top of the rise you can admire the fine views on the right (southward) before turning left through bushes and a gate. Then turn right and continue with a hedge now on your right towards a wooden house. Continue along a hedged path with the house on your left ignoring a stile on the right. Cross a bridge in a dip and follow the hedged path up to a road.

Here turn rightwards for 100 yards and then go leftwards on a narrow

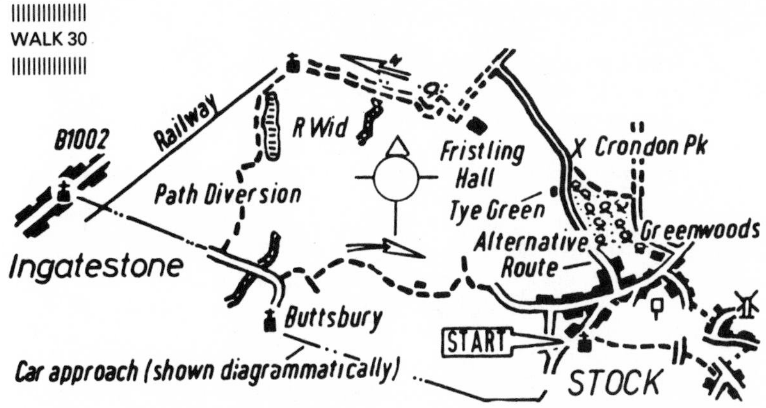

path to the right of a house (No. 25 on garage) between a beech hedge and conifers. There is a telephone pole at the entrance. Cross a stile and go across a meadow to the right-hand corner of hedge opposite and then on, half right, to a stile in the middle of a wire fence ahead and about 25 yards to the right of a brick house. Continue on the path past a cottage on the right and out to Madles Lane.

Turn left and shortly, at a T-junction, left again. In only a few yards turn rightwards on a track at the far end of a house named 'Siljan'. Have this house on your right as you follow out to a lane opposite Stockwell House.

Here turn left with views of the windmill to your right and then take the first right turn (Mill Lane) and continue to the windmill. Having inspected it at close quarters retrace your way along Mill Lane and in a couple of hundred yards turn rightwards on a grassy track by the side of Windmill Chase.

The walk follows a grassy track with a hedge and ditch on the left. Pass a seat on the right and the end of a housing estate road and on along a path to the left of house No. 34 to a road. Turn rightwards, past a cricket field and the Bakers Arms on the left and so out to the main road. Here turn rightwards and immediately past the end of a wall beyond 'Greenwoods' on the left turn left in Crondon Park Lane (with impressive views towards Galley Wood church half-right ahead). Where the wood on your left ends (rather over ¼ mile from the main road) cross (or go through) a bar stile on the left (on my visit I found barbed wire on the top rail) and then go downhill with a wood on the left. In the dip I found, on my visit, rather swampy conditions as the streamlet (ditch) here was clogged up and causing an overflow (larger scale maps show a spring adjacent). I understand that the West Essex Group of the Ramblers' Association have noted this fact and hope, given the necessary consent of the landowner and the co-operation of the Chelmsford District Council, to be able to clear the ditch and to construct a footbridge. If on your visit you do find such a bridge here, spare a thought for those who *care* about these things.

It is possible to detour a little to a spot where the ditch is narrower and can be jumped, but in a book of this kind I cannot describe anything but the legal right of way (or, occasionally, what might be reasonably regarded as long-standing permissive use).

In case of difficulty — note, from the sketch map, that point X can be reached by retracing a little of your way and taking a lane from Stock. But if you can cross the ditch proceed as follows:

Where the wood recedes to the left keep straight on, hedge on left, over a crossing path and on to the top of a rise. Here bear left to a road on the left (point X). Here turn rightwards, very soon to pass and disregard the drive of Fristling Hall on your left. (In theory you should come out on to the lane at a point opposite the drive.)

Continue in the lane for ½ mile with fine views all around to where it makes a square, right bend. Here turn left on a green track signposted as a public bridleway. In a short ½ mile you pass and disregard a track coming in leftwards from Fristling Hall. (In Essex 'Hall' usually means a farm not the manor-type house usually associated with the term.) About 150 yards past this turn squarely right (*don't* continue ahead) on a track that soon reaches a wood and then bears left-right round its corner and then runs alongside it. There are delightful views over the Wid valley to Margaretting and to Ingatestone churches.

Continue over the little river Wid and so to Margaretting church which stands some way south-west of the village. Pass the church on your left and continue on a track signposted 'Courtesy Footpath' to Stock Road with the railway on your right. In the dip cross the bridge and turn left by a second courtesy footpath signpost. Follow the hedge on your left with views to the left over the reservoir until you reach a transverse concrete track by a gate on the left. Turn right to a crossroads of concrete tracks and turn left by a third courtesy footpath signpost passing storage tanks on your left. Follow the track to a lane. The official path (No. 43) runs to the east of the track you are now using (indeed you pass the signpost and entry to it just after reaching the lane).

Turn left in the lane so reached, soon recrossing the river Wid. Where, ¼ mile farther on, the road bends right, turn left up a track headed with a 'No Through Road' sign. The track soon bend rightwards and then, in another 100 or so yards, *left*. It swings round gradually in a wide curve (note again, the fine views to the west) and in nearly a mile from the road, passes between the farm buildings of Imphy Hall, with the house itself on the left. Disregard a track running squarely left but keep forward, soon passing a large pond on your left. On meeting a transverse track turn rightwards. In ¼ mile this runs out to a lane and you pass Lane End Cottage on the left. Keep on this lane, ignoring footpath offshoots to the right for about ¾ mile. Then turn rightwards on a little lane. Follow to the B1007 and here turn left, very soon to Stock church again.